STAND
FOR

JOHN ENSOR & SCOTT KLUSENDORF

STAND
FOR
LIFE

HENDRICKSON
PUBLISHERS

Stand for Life: A Student's Guide for Making the Case and Saving Lives

© 2012 by Hendrickson Publishers Marketing, LLC
P. O. Box 3473
Peabody, Massachusetts 01961-3473

ISBN 978-1-61970-117-5

First Hendrickson Edition Printing — November 2012

Library of Congress Cataloging-in-Publication

A catalog record for this book is available
from the Library of Congress
Hendrickson Publishers Marketing, LLC
ISBN 978-1-61970-117-5

Contents

Foreword

There's good news and bad news on the abortion front.

The good news is that abortion isn't popular. More and more people, particularly the millennials I speak to, don't *like* it. They're not impressed with euphemistic phrases like *reproductive rights* and *women's health*, both of which cover up the ugly reality of abortion on demand. Indeed, students don't have to look far to see the truth. Modern technology displays for all to see the beauty of innocent human life in the womb. Double homicide laws and other legal innovations demonstrate the inconsistency of legalized abortion on demand. Resource centers and the culture-wide embrace of adoption have established clear and compelling alternatives to abortion in cases of unplanned pregnancies.

The bad news is that many who oppose abortion lack the knowledge, skill, and practice to articulate that opposition in a winsome manner. Their hearts are passionate, but their minds lack training. As a result, the pervasive relativism that undergirds the culture of death remains largely unchallenged by Christian students. Their peers widely assume that one's position on abortion is a matter of personal choice rather than a matter of public truth.

If pro-life students are to change that, they must learn to present public arguments that can't be dismissed as private belief. If they do anything less, they will find themselves ill equipped to face pro-abortion professors and fellow students. They'll be embarrassed when forced to stand up for the unborn. Even worse, they'll be unwilling to stand for the unborn at all!

Think about it: a lack of clarity eventually erodes away courage and conviction. Thus the most significant human rights issue of our lifetime is reduced to a matter of personal preference, and the evil that is abortion remains a scourge on our society. This is especially ironic in light of how concerned we seem to be these days for causes of social justice.

I am convinced that this book provides a missing piece for the pro-life puzzle. In the chapters that follow, you will find the clear, factual, and usable arguments that pro-life defenders simply must know today. As you learn these arguments, you will also find your courage and conviction bolstered and your passion for the unborn renewed.

Why do I believe this? Because I have seen it work. I've watched Scott Klusendorf train thousands of high school and college students in these pro-life arguments. I've watched students hear the material, learn the material, and then use the material to defend life in personal conversations, academic papers, classroom debates, and the public square. John Ensor, meanwhile, has established pregnancy centers in major urban areas through the United States. These centers reach out to women at a critical juncture, when the word *positive* is the last sound they want to hear. Now John is taking his ministry overseas, equipping international pro-life advocates to stand for biblical truth against impossible odds. He's lived out his pro-life convictions in the toughest of circumstances.

I am so glad that thousands of others will now be trained because Scott and John have made this book available. We can defeat abortion. We can defend life. Let's get started.

John Stonestreet
Author and Fellow,
The Chuck Colson Center for Christian Worldview
Senior Content Adviser, Summit Ministries

Introduction

Answering the Call, Making the Case, Saving Lives

Our hope in writing this book is to put the baton in your hands and inspire you to run hard towards victory!

Some things are so wrong, so horrible even to look at, that you will quickly look away for your own emotional protection. Or, you will draw nearer, in spite of the discomfort, take a good hard look, and consider what you might do to stop it.

Welcome to the pro-life movement.

We are persuaded that legal abortion is the preeminent injustice of our times. We want to peacefully, winsomely, persuasively, and courageously speak up for the unborn child[1] until the humanity of each one is acknowledged and respected. Along the way, we are committed to helping mothers, who are at risk for abortion due to their difficult circumstances, find the practical, life-affirming help they need to parent successfully or place for adoption. Our passion is to make abortion unwanted today and unthinkable for future generations.

It's not that we only care about unborn babies. We care about all human suffering. Utilitarian ethics, the notion that some lives can be destroyed to improve the lives of others, inevitably leads to a general diminution of all human life. What justifies abortion chips away the bedrock of our national ideal, expressed in the Declaration of Independence, that "all men are created equal, that they are endowed by their Creator with certain unalienable Rights, that among these are Life, Liberty, and the pursuit of Happiness."

Why are these rights called unalienable? To remind the high and mighty that they are not that high and mighty. They are not God. And some things are gifts from God and not from any human ruler or body of rulers. What Congress can give, Congress can take away. The right to life is unalienable precisely because it's out of reach of government— whether executive, legislative, or judicial. It can be unjustly usurped and trampled upon to be sure, but not rightly so. This is what makes abortion inherently unjust. It takes away what only God can justly give and take: human life.

Do not think we always saw things so clearly. We were told that abortion means choice. Choice is another word for freedom. Hey, who can be against freedom? That was as far as our thinking went when Scott, my co-author, and I came of age in the 70's. Our generation put on our Beatles records, got into our yellow submarines and came out pretty much convinced that we invented sex, drugs, and rock and roll. The key to our newfound lifestyle, the new freedom that made it all possible, was legalized abortion in 1973.

Every lure, however, has a hook. When our generation started to "have sex" in the same way we "have a hamburger," it did not take long for us to feel the hook. We were dragged off and devoured by our choices. Then ultrasound came along and only made the truth more visible. And we have had time to think. By painful experience, when not by clear moral reasoning, we came to understand what abortion truly is and what it also does to manhood, womanhood, marriage, and the culture at large. If you have your own regrets concerning abortion, you are not alone. Nor are you a hypocrite now for re-examining your values and considering the case for life. You are growing up and learning from your mistakes like the rest of us.

The struggle over abortion is now moving into its second generation. Forty years ago, the pro-life movement consisted of a few Catholic voices crying out in the wilderness. Today, hundreds of thousands of Catholic, evangelical, Anglican, and charismatic Christians work side by side in the cause of life all over the world. Along the way, it has won over many others who do not share our Christian faith or worldview. We welcome this. Victory, after all, means that people of every faith or no faith, come to understand the injustice of abortion in the same way we have come to see the injustice of slavery. But like the struggle against slavery, the first responders have been Christians motivated by their faith.[2] Even today, it's the Christian faith, and the value of life it places on each individual, that serves as the supply line for the rapidly expanding life movement.

When we asked ourselves what you and other students who are just coming into the life movement need right away and in bite-size pieces, we came up with two answers. First, given the Christian worldview that most of you have, you need a basic understanding of the case for life according to the Bible. Your pro-life work is, in large part, an outworking of your Christian faith and practice. Therefore this book aims to ground your values and your actions in the rich soil of biblical teaching that will help you challenge the powers of death with the gospel of life and do it in a way that is both soul satisfying and God glorifying. Second, given the materialistic and humanistic worldview of the culture in which you live, you need basic training in making the case for life in a rational and winning way to a secular world.

Now logically, you might expect us to present them in that order. But we decided to flip the script. Why? Ready, aim, fire! is oversold in our view. Ready, fire, aim is actually the way the world works in most places. Getting started, engaging in great things, even when not fully prepared, helps you see what you need to learn. And we learn from experience, even from mistakes, as much as from a book.

In addition, confidence, which comes from doing, is as important to build up as competence. The world does not need highly developed pro-life theoreticians. It needs evangels, people sensing the call of God on their lives and effectively appealing to the conscience of their generation. And it needs Samaritans, ready to act on their convictions in practical lifesaving ways. You are already networked with fellow students who are only now forming their views. Engage them. Even now, the people who profit in the shedding of innocent blood are marketing their services to your fellow students. Students have more abortions than any other demographic. In other words, you are already on the frontline. Engage. Learn. Engage again. Learn more.

As you grow, graduate and move on, we hope you find your place of service in the larger pro-life movement for the long haul. You have lots of choices. Out of the hard work and generosity of the first generation of the pro-life movement, hundreds of different organizations have developed. Some are focused on your neighborhood, while others have a statewide, national, or even international mission.

Some pro-life organizations have an educational mission. Some are dedicated to exposing the violence and injustice of abortion itself. Others concentrate on educating the public about biological human development and showcase the beauty of unborn human life. Still others educate the public on the physical and psychological after-effects of abortion. Some are collecting and publishing affidavits from men and women who regret their abortion. Some address the spreading tentacles of utilitarian thinking as it reformulates into physician-assisted suicide, cloning, embryonic stem-cell research, and gendercide.

Some pro-life organizations are political and legislative in nature. They engage in the democratic process to get pro-life values represented at all levels of government. They work with legislators to draft and adopt just laws and protections that lessen abortion, until the day it can be ended altogether.

Legal abortion was justified in part as a private matter between a woman and her doctor. So pro-life medical organizations have emerged. Some focus on doctors-in-training, building up a medical immunity among their ranks to resist the pressure put on them to learn and practice abortion surgery. Others are working to restore to the medical profession the original Hippocratic oath that forswore any life-harming practices and thus perverted the healing profession into something else.

There are pro-life legal defense organizations. There are pro-life research organizations. There are pro-life clergy associations. There are organizations of pro-life writers, artists, and musicians. There are teens for life and motorcyclists for life and iPhone users for life (well, maybe not, but you could start one and even design an app!) Right where you live, you can participate in a march for life or a walk for life, even a car wash for life.

You are part of a dynamic new wave of students for life. Together you are sensing a call and you want to make a difference. We, who have been at this for twenty-some years, are familiar with this call. We can testify after these many years that it's a mighty calling and that God can and will use you to make a lifesaving difference.

You represent the next generation ready to take up this great work. This book represents two guys from the first generation training you how to run with the baton!

Who are Scott and John?

Scott is a BMOC. He routinely debates abortion-choice advocates at the university level. As the president of Life Training Institute, he trains pro-life advocates to persuasively defend their views and make the case for life rationally, winsomely, and effectively.

John is a preacher-man. He has spent the last twenty-plus years helping local churches understand the biblical call to cherish and defend innocent human life and to answer that call by establishing ultrasound-equipped pregnancy help centers in the neediest neighborhoods of our nation. Currently he serves as the President of PassionLife, a global initiative to raise up defenders of life and start pregnancy help services in the neediest places.

We've written some books (see pages 145–46) that build on all that we are introducing here. A quick Google search will tell you how helpful others have found these books. In this book, our goal is to introduce you to the basics and encourage you to speak and act confidently right now. The case for life is right and true. More than that, it's a lifesaving power. Many of your generation believe that with faith toward God and hard work, the inhumanity of legal abortion can end on your watch. That would be a historic, God-glorifying legacy. Better get started!

Chapter 1

Defending Your Pro-Life Views in Five Minutes or Less

There is no relevant difference between the embryo you once were and the young adult that you are today that would justify killing you at that earlier stage of development.

Suppose that you have just five minutes to graciously defend your pro-life beliefs with friends or classmates. Can you do it with rational arguments? What should you say? And how can you begin simplifying the abortion issue for those who think it's hopelessly complex?

Here's how to succeed in three steps:

1. Clarify the issue.

Pro-life advocates contend that elective abortion unjustly takes the life of a defenseless human being. This simplifies the abortion controversy by focusing public attention on just one question: Is the unborn a member of the human family? If so, killing him or her to benefit others is a serious moral wrong. It treats the distinct human being, with his or her own inherent moral worth, as nothing more than a disposable instrument. Conversely, if the unborn are not human, killing them for any reason requires no more justification than having a tooth pulled.

In other words, arguments based on "choice" or "privacy" miss the point entirely. Would anyone that you know support a mother killing her toddler in the name of "choice and who decides?" Clearly, if the unborn are human, like toddlers, we shouldn't kill them in the name of choice anymore than we would a toddler. Again, this debate is about just one question: What is the unborn? At this point, some may object that your comparisons are not fair—that killing a fetus is morally different than killing a toddler. Ah, but that's the issue, isn't it? Are the unborn, like toddlers, members of the human family? That is the one issue that matters.

Remind your critics that you are vigorously "pro-choice" when it comes to women choosing a number of moral goods. You support a woman's right to choose her own doctor, to choose her own husband, to choose her own job, and to choose her own religion, to name a few. These are among the many choices that you fully support for women. But some choices are wrong, like killing innocent human beings simply because they are in the way and cannot defend themselves.[1] No, we shouldn't be allowed to choose that.

2. Defend your pro-life position with science and philosophy.

The science of embryology tells us that from the earliest stages of development, the unborn are distinct, living, and whole human beings. Leading embryology books confirm this.[2] For example, Keith L. Moore and T. V. N. Persaud write, "A zygote is the beginning of a new human being. Human development begins at fertilization, the process during which a male gamete or sperm . . . unites with a female gamete or oocyte . . . to form a single cell called a zygote. This highly specialized, totipotent cell marks the beginning of each of us as a unique individual."[3] Prior to his abortion advocacy, former Planned Parenthood president Dr. Alan Guttmacher was perplexed that anyone, much less a medical doctor, would question this. "This all seems so simple and evident that it is difficult to picture a time when it wasn't part of the common knowledge," he wrote in his book *Life in the Making*.[4]

Philosophically, we can say that embryos are less developed than newborns (or, for that matter, toddlers), but this difference is not morally significant in the way abortion advocates need it to be. Consider the claim that the immediately exercisable capacity for self-awareness bestows value on human beings, and embryos lack that capacity. Notice that this is not an argument, but an arbitrary assertion. Why is some development needed? And why is this particular degree of development (i.e., higher brain function) decisive rather than another? These are questions that abortion advocates do not adequately address.

As philosophy professor Stephen Schwarz points out, there is no morally significant difference between the embryo that you once were and the adult that you are today that would justify killing you at that early stage of development. Differences of size, level of development, environment, and degree of dependency are not relevant such that we can say that you had no rights as an embryo but you do have rights today.[5] Schwarz suggests the acronym SLED as a helpful reminder of these nonessential differences:

Size: True, embryos are smaller than newborns and adults, but why is that relevant? Do we really want to say that large people are more human than small ones? Men are generally larger than women, but that doesn't mean that they deserve more rights. Size doesn't equal value.

Level of Development: True, embryos and fetuses are less developed than the adults they'll one day become. But again, why is this relevant? Four-year-old girls are less developed than fourteen-year-old ones. Should older children have more rights than their younger siblings? Some people say that self-awareness makes one human. But if that is true, newborns do not qualify as valuable human beings. Six-week old infants lack the immediately exercisable capacity for performing human mental functions, as do the reversibly comatose, the sleeping, and those with Alzheimer's Disease. Like the early embryo, a man in a reversible coma has the natural capacity for mental functions even if he can't presently exercise them.

Environment: Where you are has no bearing on who you are. Does your value change when you cross the street or roll over in bed? If not, how can a journey of eight inches down the birth canal suddenly change the essential nature of the unborn from non-human to human? If the unborn are not already human, merely changing their location can't make them valuable.

Degree of Dependency: If viability makes us human, then all those who depend on insulin or kidney medication are not valuable and we may kill them. Conjoined twins who share blood type and bodily systems also have no right to life.

In short, it's far more reasonable to argue that although humans differ immensely with respect to talents, accomplishments, and degrees of development, they are nonetheless equal because they share a common human nature.

3. Challenge your listeners to be intellectually honest.

Ask the tough questions. When critics say that birth makes the unborn human, ask, "How does a mere change of location from inside the womb to outside the womb change the essential nature of the unborn?" If they say that brain development or self-awareness makes us human, ask if they would agree that those with an IQ below 40 or perhaps 60 should be declared nonpersons? If not, why not? True, some people will ignore the scientific and philosophic case you present for the pro-life view and argue for abortion based on self-interest. That is the lazy way out. Remind your critics that if we care about truth, we will courageously follow a good argument wherever it leads, no matter what the cost to our own self-interests.

Let's toughen the job. Suppose you only get one minute to make your pro-life case. Now what? Don't panic. Just summarize what's stated above. Here's how:

Either you believe that each and every human being has an equal right to life or you don't. The science of embryology tells us that from the earliest stages of development, the unborn are distinct, living, and whole human beings. Sure, they have yet to mature, but they are whole human beings just the same. Philosophically, there is no essential difference between the embryo you once were and the adult you are today that would justify killing you at that earlier stage. Differences of size, level of development, environment, and degree of dependency are not good reasons for saying you could be killed then but not now.

Chapter 2

Understanding Why We Speak of the Sanctity of Human Life

There is no relevant difference between the embryo you once were and the young adult you are today that would remove your life from God's love and protection.

Dr. Bernard Nathanson (1926–2011) wrote, "I am personally responsible for over seventy-five thousand abortions."[1] He was one of the main architects of the strategic plan to dehumanize the unborn child and legitimize abortion across the country.[2] He succeeded beyond all his own expectations.

Then something happened that forced him to see abortion for what it is and to renounce all that he had done and advocated. Ultrasound technology arrived in his office in the midseventies. Ultrasound provided a true "window to the womb" and revealed the humanity of the unborn child. Nathanson wrote:

From then on we could see this person in the womb from the very beginning—and study and measure it and weigh it and take care of it and treat it and diagnose it and do all kinds of things. It became, in essence, a second patient. Now a patient is a person. So basically I was dealing then with two people, instead of just one carrying some lump of meat around. That's what started me doubting the ethical acceptability of abortion on request.[3]

Dr. Nathanson's acknowledgment of the humanity of the unborn child had no conscious religious tone to it. He was an atheistic Jew. "I had not a seedling of faith to nourish me," he wrote.[4] Embryology itself, confirmed by ultrasound, led him to acknowledge that there was no significant difference between the humanity of the mother and that of her unborn child, that would justify killing her baby.

In 1983, *The New England Journal of Medicine* reported that ultrasound was reshaping the whole medical profession; that doctors need to see the unborn child as a patient.

Ultrasound imagery will probably change the way in which we view the fetus with a diagnosed and treatable disorder. . . . Indeed, surgeons already regard the fetus with a correctable congenital defect as a "patient."[5]

The same report also indicated that ultrasound examinations were turning ambivalent mothers toward parenthood and away from abortion.

One of us pointed to the small, visibly moving fetal form on the screen and asked, "How do you feel about seeing what is inside you?" She answered crisply, "It certainly makes you think twice about abortion! . . . I

feel that it is human. It belongs to me. I could never
have an abortion now."

"The truth will out," wrote Shakespeare. The truth of
our humanity in the early stages of our development, along
with all of its beauty and wonder, has been outed by ultrasound. Opening this window to the womb is clearing away
the obfuscation and moral fog required to justify abortion.
As a result, the tide is turning.
Opinion polls taken in the U.S. over the past twenty
years have shown a tick, tick, ticking swing toward the pro-
life position. A May 2009 Gallup Poll found 51 percent of
Americans calling themselves "pro-life" on the issue of abortion and 42 percent "pro-choice." This was the first time a
majority of U.S. adults have identified themselves as pro-life
since Gallup began asking the question in 1995. Another
national survey by the Pew Research Center taken about the
same time, showed an 8 percentage-point decline from a
survey taken in 2008, among those saying abortion should
be legal in all or most cases. This view went from a majority 54 percent to a minority of 46 percent. The percentage
saying abortion should be legal in only a few or no cases
increased from 41 to 44 over the same period.[6]
Forty years after the right to abortion was identified
in the "penumbra of the constitution" by a few men on the
Supreme Court, the practice is by no means settled. In fact,
it grows more unsettling to us with each passing year. Why?
Part of the answer is that every day thousands of women
and couples show up for their routine ultrasounds. They go
home clutching pictures of their own unborn children and
then sending them to family and friends.
Yes, the child is small. It definitely has a big head in
proportion to the rest of its body. It's less developed than it
will be, a week later, a month later and certainly ten years

later. It's moving about in an environment common to us all, yet strangely new for us to look in and observe. Though it's dependent on mom for nourishment, as it will be after birth, yet what we see on the ultrasound, even to the untrained eye, looks near enough to us as human that our sympathy and love are naturally aroused.

We respond as normal, healthy people always do—with a tender and willing desire to provide and protect this little one. (We always protect what we love.) Ultrasound is helping us think more clearly and react the same way we would respond if we were watching a two-year-old toddler on a security camera and then saw someone coming at her with a knife. We would run to her aid and defense.

Ultrasound, however, is not the only window to the womb. The Bible, too, is a source of revelation. It, too, reveals the truth of our humanity. It, too, confirms that there is no relevant difference between the embryo you once were and the young adult that you are today that would justify killing you at that earlier stage of development. And it, too, reveals how God protects what he loves.

Since many of your fellow students do not accept the Bible as an authoritative source of truth, simply quoting Scripture will not settle the matter. On the other hand, you can bet your Starbucks chai macchiato latte that if the Bible *did* make a distinction between the embryo you once were and the young adult you have become that would justify killing you in the early stages of development, they would quote it to you. So consistency is important.

It's important for at least four reasons. First, it's important for you to know. You need to know that some things rest on an even firmer foundation than human reasoning. Some ethical demands come from a higher authority than any government laws or executive order or judicial decree. Human rights come from above. When the two are in conflict, sides must be taken and courage must be found. Very few things in this world are worth fighting for. But oh! How precious those few things are! Innocent human life is one of them.

This is why we speak of the sanctity of human life. We assert that all human life is sacred and belongs to God because all people are made in the image of God (Genesis 1:27). Since every human being is created by God and in his image, every human being has intrinsic rather than relative value. Every human being has a natural right to life that is to be respected within a community and protected by the laws of a just society. "Give justice to the weak and the fatherless; maintain the rights of the afflicted and the destitute" (Psalm 82:3). A just society does just that. Herein lies the offense of abortion. It devalues and dehumanizes into "a product of conception" what God calls his most treasured gift—human life made in his image and designed to reflect his glory and goodness.

So there is no relevant difference between the embryo you once were and the young adult you are today that would remove your life from God's love and protection. Nor is there anything then that should remove our love and protection from our neighbor's life.

There is a second reason for us to see the humanity of the unborn child affirmed in the Scriptures. For every student who dismisses the Bible out of hand, there is another that is fully persuaded that it's the authoritative word of God. Those who take their Christian faith seriously will be interested in learning how and where God affirms the value of every human life, at all stages of development. Otherwise they are apt to think of abortion as merely an issue rather than an affront to the integrity of God.

Then there are the students on your campus who don't know yet what they believe about God or life, or a host of major issues. Their default position (the uncritical, unreflective position) will be to go-along and get-along. "If it's legal, it must be right" they will say. Or they have thought only as far as the bumper sticker: My body/My choice. They have yet to think through the implications of that statement. The antireligious nature of our politically correct campus culture causes these students to be slightly embarrassed and hesitant to openly say that what the Bible affirms is important to them. In spite of this, they do carry a general reverence for God. What the Bible affirms is meaningful to them. So use it.

Finally you need to understand what the Bible affirms about human life, including life in the womb because the word of God has its own power to persuade. It brings its own conviction. "The word of God is living and active, sharper than any two-edged sword, piercing to the division of soul and of spirit, of joints and of marrow, and discerning the thoughts and intentions of the heart" (Hebrews 4:12).

So where and how does the Bible affirm our essential value as human beings at the earliest stages of development?

In Genesis 4:1 we read, "Now Adam knew Eve his wife, and she conceived and bore Cain." Notice, it was the person, Cain, who was conceived and the person, Cain, who was born. Dr. John Davis, professor of theology at Gordon-Conwell Theological Seminary, observes, "The writer's interest in Cain extends back beyond his birth, to his conception. That is when his personal history begins."[7] From the moment of conception, the humanity—the life—of Cain began.

The same is true of Job's life. He also saw his personal history as beginning at conception. He said, "Let the day perish on which I was born, and the night that said, 'A man is conceived'" (Job 3:3). He was in the pit of despair when he cried these words. His personal suffering and loss was immeasurable. Perhaps you have also felt such agonizing loss and grief in your own life, that you wished that you had not been born to experience it. If so, you understand Job's cry. Nonetheless look at how he sees his life before God, his Creator. What was conceived? Not a potential man, something abstract or short of humanity, but a man (human) was conceived.

Clifford Bajema said it succinctly, "Scripture does not make the kind of subtle philosophical distinctions people make so often today between human life and human being, man and person, life and Life. Scripture just talks about man."[8]

So we read in Genesis 25:22 about Rebekah, "The children struggled together within her." Throughout the Old Testament, this Hebrew word for children (*benim*) is the same word used for children outside the womb.

In the New Testament we observe the same perspective: human life is human life, inside or outside the womb. Right after the angel Gabriel announced to Mary that she would conceive by the power of the Holy Spirit, we read that Mary went "with haste" to visit Elizabeth. "In those days Mary arose and went with haste into the hill country, to a town in Judah, and she entered the house of Zechariah and greeted Elizabeth" (Luke 1:39–40). Elizabeth herself was six months pregnant with the unborn child who we will come to know as John the Baptist. Depending on how far the walk was, one or two days, maybe three or four—let's give her a week, even walking with haste—the point is that Mary is in the earliest days of her pregnancy and Jesus is, in biological terms, a zygote. When Mary meets Elizabeth, Jesus is probably not yet implanted in the womb. But level of development and location does not determine our humanity.

The preborn child, John, reacts to being in the presence of the fully divine and fully human unborn, and very tiny (less than the size of a pinhead), almighty Son of God. We read,

When Elizabeth heard the greeting of Mary, the baby leaped in her womb. And Elizabeth was filled with the Holy Spirit, and she exclaimed with a loud cry, "Blessed are you among women, and blessed is the fruit of your womb! And why is this granted to me that the mother of my Lord should come to me? For behold, when the sound of your greeting came to my ears, the baby in my womb leaped for joy" (Luke 1:41–44).

When the two mothers meet, a little womb-to-womb praise and worship service begins. This by itself is a powerful affirmation of the humanity of unborn children. But we also observe that the word "baby" (the Greek word *brephos*) used in the phrase, "baby in my womb" is the same word used in Luke 2:12 and 2:16 for the newborn baby Jesus: "You will find a baby wrapped in swaddling cloths and lying in a manger."

In the worldview of the Bible, children are children whether inside a womb or inside a house. Environment does not determine human value, any more than size or level of development or dependence. When a mother announces, "I am having a baby," she is reflecting God's own view of it.

Chapter 3

Simplifying the Abortion Debate in a Moral Fog

Despite what you've heard, the abortion debate is not complex. One question clarifies everything.

Let's jump twelve years into the future. You're in your thirties, married, and have a five-year-old boy. One day as you're scrubbing dishes with your back turned, he enters the kitchen and asks, "Daddy (or Mommy), can I kill this?" What are the first words out of your mouth? You can never answer the question "Can I kill this?" until you answer the underlying question, what is it?[1]

Gregory Koukl writes, "Abortion involves killing and discarding something that's alive. Whether or not it's right to take the life of any living thing depends entirely on the question what it is."[2] As stated in chapter 1, pro-life advocates contend that elective abortion is the intentional killing of a defenseless human being. They argue their case in two steps. First, they use the science of embryology to establish the humanity of the unborn. Second, they argue from philosophy that each member of the human family has an equal right to life. In short, pro-life advocates present an *argument* for their position. Their opponents, however, sometimes look for a short cut.

The Problem: Assuming What They Are Trying to Prove

Most advocates of elective abortion deny the unborn are fully human. But here's the trick: Instead of proving that conclusion with facts and arguments, many just assume it within the course of their rhetoric. We call this "begging the question" and, as philosopher Francis J. Beckwith points out, it's a logical fallacy that lurks behind many arguments for abortion.[3]

For example, consider the claim that laws against abortion will force women into the back alleys of America, where they will die at the hands of illegal abortionists. We'll unpack this assertion in chapter 11, but notice it assumes the unborn are not human. Otherwise, the claim amounts to this: Because some humans will die attempting to kill others, the state should make it safe and legal for them to do so. But why should the law be faulted for making it more risky for one human to take the life of another completely innocent one? Thus, only by assuming the unborn are not human does the back-alley argument carry any force whatsoever.

Or suppose you're told that reproductive freedom means the ability to choose whether or not to have children according to one's own personal religious beliefs. That freedom is necessary, so the argument goes, so all humans can lead lives of self-determination, opportunity, and human dignity.

Notice the question-begging nature of the claim. First, the abortion-choice advocate simply assumes the pregnant woman doesn't already have a child.

But isn't that the very question under dispute in the abortion debate? After all, pro-life advocates contend the woman does indeed have a child, an unborn one—the only question is what she will do with him. Second, would this same abortion-choice advocate argue for human freedom and self-determination if the debate were about killing toddlers instead of fetuses? Never in a million years. Only by assuming the unborn are not human does the claim work. Third, if "all humans" deserve opportunity and dignity, does that include the unborn? If not, aren't we assuming something here? Thus, at every turn, the above claim for reproductive freedom begs the question by assuming the unborn are not one of us. Yet nowhere is that assumption argued for.

During a 2010 debate, Pennsylvania State Senator Daylin Leach accused me [Scott] of not trusting women to make their own personal decisions. He turned to the audience and said (paraphrase), "Scott thinks he knows better than the women of this country what's right for them. He wants government involved in their personal choices."

When it was my turn, I began by saying that I agreed with everything the senator just said. I agreed that we should trust women to make their own personal decisions. I agreed government should stay out of the decision to abort. I agreed that pro-lifers like me should butt out of this debate. In short, I agreed completely—if. If what? If the unborn are not human. And if Senator Leach could present scientific evidence to show that the unborn are not members of the human family and philosophic evidence to show that even if they are, we have no duty to value them, I would concede. In short, I was willing to buy his argument for trusting women, but only after he demonstrated the unborn are not human. I then asked the audience to consider this question: Would the senator's claim that we should "trust" women work as a justification for killing toddlers? If not, what is he assuming about the unborn that he's not assuming about the toddler? That's right, he's assuming that they are not human, like toddlers are. But he needs to argue for this, not merely assume it. Of course, the senator never did argue for his assumption.

The Fix: Trot Out a Toddler

Suppose that instead of a public debate, you're having a private conversation with your friend Jerome. He justifies elective abortion this way: "Women have a right to make their own private decisions. What goes on in the bedroom is their business and no one else's." When you hear this, don't panic. Ask yourself a simple question: Would this justification for abortion work for killing a toddler? If not, Jerome is assuming the unborn are not human. To help him see the problem, trot out a toddler:

You: Jerome, you say that privacy is the issue. Pretend that I have a two-year-old in front of me. (You hold out your hand at waist level to illustrate this.) May I kill him as long as I do it in the privacy of the bedroom?

Jerome: That's silly—of course not!

You: Why not?

Jerome: Because he's a human being.

You: Ah. If the unborn are human, like the toddler, we shouldn't kill the unborn in the name of privacy any more than we'd kill a toddler for that reason.

Jerome: But that's different. You're comparing apples with oranges, two things that are completely unrelated. Look, killing toddlers is one thing. Killing a fetus that is not a human being is quite another.

You: Ah. That's the issue, isn't it? Are the unborn human beings, like toddlers? That is the one issue that matters.

Staying on Message

Notice that you haven't argued for the humanity of the unborn. You'll do that later. For now, all you are doing is framing the discussion around one key question: What is the unborn? When pro-life advocates stay focused on that issue, the result is clarity:

Jerome: But many poor women cannot afford to raise another child.

You: When human beings get expensive, may we kill them? Getting back to my toddler example, suppose a large family collectively decides to quietly dispose of its three youngest children to help ease the family budget. Is that okay?

Jerome: Well, no, but aborting a fetus is not the same as killing children.

You: So, once again, the issue is: What is the unborn? Is the fetus the same as a human being? We can't escape that question, can we?

Jerome: But what about a woman who's been raped? Every time she looks at that kid she's going to remember what happened to her. If that's not hardship, what is?

You: I agree that we should provide compassionate care for the victim, and it should be the best care possible. That's not at issue here. It's your proposed solution I'm struggling to understand. Tell me, how should a civil society treat innocent human beings that remind us of a painful event? Is it okay to kill them so we can feel better? Can we, for example, kill a toddler who reminds her mother of a rape?

Jerome: No, I wouldn't do that.

You: I wouldn't either. But again, isn't that because you and I both agree that it's wrong to kill innocent human beings, even if they do remind us of a painful event?

Jerome: But you don't understand how much this woman has suffered. Put yourself in her shoes. How would you feel?

You: You're right. I don't understand her feelings. How could I? How could anyone? I'm just asking if hardship justifies homicide? Can we, for instance, kill toddlers who remind us of painful events? Again, my claim here is really quite modest. If the unborn are members of the human family, like toddlers, we should not kill them to make someone else feel better.

Perhaps now Jerome will listen to your pro-life arguments based on science and philosophy. (See chapter 1.) But don't go there until you clarify the one question that really matters.

Chapter 4

Developing a Christian Response to Abortion

Answering one question clarifies the demands of love.

Answering the one question, "what is it?" clarifies the abortion debate for the most part. A challenge remains. Sin corrupts our thinking. It sidesteps logic. It bends our thoughts toward what most protects our sinful self-interest. The apostle Paul put it this way, "Unrighteousness suppresses the truth" (Romans 1:18).

For forty years now, abortion has been legal and accessible. With an estimated 45 million abortions every year worldwide, it's the defining experience of this generation. Every one of us has been affected by abortion. We have a personal experience with it or we have family and friends who have. This experience affects our thinking. It creates a cognitive dissonance that resists the truth. "Abortion must not kill children because I would never kill a child; yet I had (or encouraged) an abortion."

Remember this, as you are talking to people. You are using truth and reason, but you are using it to cut through self-deception and self-justification. Be clear, but be patient.

Asking the question, "what is it?" also clarifies for us our own moral responsibility as Christians regarding the injustice of abortion. A professor of mine once tried to dismiss this obligation by quipping: "The Bible doesn't even mention the word *abortion*."

This is true. Of course the Bible doesn't mention drunken driving or domestic violence either. It doesn't use the word *genocide*. Does that mean the Bible is silent as to the evil and injustice of genocide? The Bible doesn't explicitly forbid the killing of professors either. Yet if I propose that we call it "professor-cide" and legalize it, he would all of a sudden gain the moral clarity he lacks when it comes to the defenseless and voiceless unborn child. His self-interest would blow away the moral fog and he would argue, "The Bible condemns professor-cide by condemning homicide and by affirming that there is no difference between professors and any other people that would justify killing them." In arguing this way, he is merely demanding that we ask, "what is it?" before we approve killing it.

What is the unborn? It's a human being. To kill the unborn is just another form of homicide, or what the Bible condemns as the shedding of innocent blood (e.g., Deuteronomy 19:10; Proverbs 6:16–17; James 5:5–6).[1]

How does God respond to the shedding of innocent blood? How does he teach us to respond to it?

In Genesis 4:10, God refers to blood as a vivid way of speaking for human life itself. Cain murders his brother Abel, and God says to Cain, "What have you done? The voice of your brother's blood is crying to me from the ground." Blood is here described as having a voice and crying out because blood in this context, stands for life itself. Elsewhere we read,

"The life of every creature is its blood: its blood is its life" (Leviticus 17:14). Blood has unique, life-giving properties. It is therefore an apt metaphor for the value of life itself.

What then is God's response to cheapening and destroying what he holds of supreme value?

1. God hears the cries of the innocent.

Abel's blood cried out to God, and God heard this cry. Everyone who has suffered violence can take comfort in this. As the psalmist says,

> Sing praises to the LORD, who sits enthroned in Zion!
>   Tell among the peoples his deeds!
> For he who avenges blood is mindful of them;
>   he does not forget the cry of the afflicted
>   (Psalm 9:11–12).

2. God vindicates the afflicted and avenges the guilty.

God vindicates the afflicted and avenges those who shed innocent blood. He vindicated the life of Abel by passing judgment on Cain. "And now you are cursed from the ground, which has opened its mouth to receive your brother's blood from your hand" (Genesis 4:11).

Judgment is the message of the prophets. Consider the prophet Ezekiel: "Thus says the Lord God: A city that sheds blood in her midst . . . You have become guilty by the blood you have shed" (Ezekiel 22:3–4).

Because God loves, he gets angry. Consider the prophet Isaiah:

> When you spread out your hands,
>   I will hide my eyes from you;

even though you make many prayers,
>   I will not listen;
>   your hands are full of blood.
> Wash yourselves;
>   make yourselves clean (Isaiah 1:15–16).

God cherishes innocent human life with a burning heart. He commands all men and women everywhere to do the same. His revulsion at the murder of the innocents knows no limit, nor does his wrath when it's finally unleashed.

God's wrath is called fierce (1 Samuel 28:18), furious (Job 40:11), full (Psalm 78:38), consuming (Psalm 59:13), great (Psalm 102:10), and jealous (Ezekiel 36:6). For God to warn us of his wrath is another sign of his love. For us to ignore it is a sign of how hardened we have become. To such people God says, "You have fattened your hearts in a day of slaughter. You have condemned and murdered the righteous person. He does not resist you" (James 5:5–6). We will look further at God's just condemnation for the shedding of innocent blood at the end of the book. It raises the obvious questions to which the Christian faith—the hope of the gospel—addresses to all mankind: is there any hope for forgiveness? If so, on what basis can God forgive sin and still vindicate the victims? How can I be reconciled to God?

For now, let's just affirm that God is right to be angry. We too protect what we love. We too are enflamed when those we love are murdered.

Developing a Christian response to the shedding of innocent blood.

Asking the question, "what is it?" also clarifies for us our own moral responsibility as Christians regarding the injustice of abortion. How does God want us to respond to the shedding of innocent blood? I would summarize the biblical ethic this way:

Negatively, we are not to shed blood or passively watch others shed innocent blood.

Positively, we are to rescue and defend the innocent.

Both of these obligations can be further reduced to one Great Commandment. "Love your neighbor as yourself" (Leviticus 19:18). The apostle Paul enlarges the point: "The commandments, 'You shall not commit adultery, You shall not murder, You shall not steal, You shall not covet,' and any other commandment, are summed up in this word: 'You shall love your neighbor as yourself.' Love does no wrong to a neighbor; therefore love is the fulfilling of the law" (Romans 13:9–10).

In other words, we fulfill the actual obligations of the Ten Commandments, including, "You shall not murder" (Exodus 20:13) by earnestly heeding the Great Commandment: "Love your neighbor."

Jesus, of course, affirmed the lifesaving power of neighborly love in his parable of the Good Samaritan (Luke 10:25–37). A man fell among robbers who "stripped him and beat him and departed, leaving him half dead" (10:30). They are obviously guilty of shedding innocent blood. But the passive acceptance of death as shown by the priest and the Levite are equally condemned. They did not administer the deadly beating. But they accepted it. They did nothing to intervene and preserve life. They "saw him" but "passed by on the other side" (10:31, 32).

We see the same positive and negative command concerning human life elsewhere in Scripture. In Deuteronomy 21:1–9, God instructs the people of Israel how to respond when they find a man murdered in their midst and it's not known who did it. The leaders of the town nearest to the body are required to summon all the people together. They are required to lead the whole community through a rather expensive ritual involving good commercial land and the sacrifice of an expensive piece of livestock. All this is designed to help them feel economically what they would normally feel emotionally if anyone knew the slain man. But they don't. So this ritual is designed to help them feel that loss as God feels it, for he was not a stranger to God.

Gathered together then, the leaders are to retouch the moral bricks of the community. Through prayer, they remind everyone of the moral responsibility they bear to cherish and defend innocent human life. They are taught to pray two things:

1. "Our hands did not shed this blood," and

2. "nor did our eyes see it shed" (Deuteronomy 21:7).

The need for the first prayer is obvious. It reminds everyone of God's law: "You shall not murder" (Exodus 20:13). But the second prayer reminds them that implicit in the command to not take human life is the obligation also to preserve human life when and how possible. Praying corporately, "We did not shed this blood, nor did we see it done" reminds them all that if they did see it happening, they were obligated to prevent it if possible.

Shedding innocent blood is abhorrent. But passive acceptance of the murder of the innocent is equally abhorrent. This of course is the central tenet of the pro-choice movement. It does not require you to personally practice abortion. It just requires you to passively accept it. When someone says, "I personally oppose abortion, but I would not tell others not to do it," they are affirming that abortion is the killing of human life but cowardly accepting it.

Passive acceptance is precisely what is condemned in Deuteronomy 21. It is also what Christ is condemning in the parable of the Good Samaritan. The priest and the Levite did not beat up the man they saw dying. But they did nothing to prevent him from dying either. As many spiritual leaders do today, the priest and the Levite could make an argument that they are pro-life. They could readily say, "We absolutely oppose beating a man and leaving him to die." But the point of the parable is that such an attitude is not pro-life. Stopping the innocent from dying is what makes you pro-life. Love is a life-preserving, death-defying power. It compels people to practical and personal solutions in the protection and care of human life.

Jesus pointed to the lifesaving actions of the Samaritan and said: "Go and do likewise." This positive command to rescue the innocent from death is repeated elsewhere. Psalm 82:3–4 says:

Give justice to the weak and the fatherless;
  maintain the right of the afflicted and the destitute.
Rescue the weak and the needy;
  deliver them from the hand of the wicked.

Eva Fogalman, in her book *Conscience and Courage: Rescuers of Jews during the Holocaust*, gives us a glorious example of what it means to cherish and defend innocent human life.

In 1942, Wladyslaw Misiuna, a teenager from Radom, Poland, was recruited by the Germans to help inmates at the Fila Majdanek concentration camp start a rabbit farm to supply furs for soldiers at the Russian front. Wladyslaw felt responsible for the thirty young women he supervised. He stuffed his coat pockets with bread, milk, carrots, and pilfered potatoes and smuggled the food to them. But one day one of his workers, Devora Salzberg, contracted a mysterious infection. Wladyslaw was beside himself. He knew if the Germans discovered the open lesions on her arms they would kill her. Wladyslaw knew that to save Devora he needed to cure her. But how? He took the simplest route. He infected himself with her blood and went to a doctor in town. The doctor prescribed a medication, which Wladyslaw then shared with Devora. Both were cured, and both survived the war.[2]

When I ask myself what it is about this story that glorifies God and satisfies my soul, I think of several reasons. Misiuna chose good over evil. He demonstrated a clear commitment to cherish and defend innocent human life. He showed great moral courage. He was practical yet creative in his lifesaving plan. Over all this, his actions imitate the very gospel of Jesus Christ. "Greater love has no one than this, that someone lays down his life for his friends" (John 15:13).

In contrast, consider another story from the same troubled time. In *The Hiding Place*, Corrie ten Boom writes of the time when her family had taken in a young Jewish mother and her baby. When the local pastor came calling, Corrie put the great test before him:

> "Would you be willing to take a Jewish mother and her baby into your home? They will almost certainly be arrested otherwise."

> Color drained from the man's face. He took a step back from me. "Miss Ten Boom! I do hope you're not involved with any of this illegal concealment and undercover business. It's just not safe! Think of your father! And your sister, she's never been strong!"

On impulse I told the pastor to wait and ran upstairs.
. . . I asked the mother's permission to borrow the in-
fant. . . . Back in the dining room I pulled back the cov-
erlet from the baby's face.

There was a long silence. The man bent forward, his
hand in spite of himself reaching for the tiny fist curled
round the blanket. For a moment I saw compassion
and fear struggle in his face. Then he straightened.
"No. Definitely not. We could lose our lives for that
Jewish child!"

Unseen by either of us, Father had appeared in the
doorway. "Give the child to me, Corrie," he said.

Father held the baby close, his white beard brushing its
cheek. . . . At last he looked up at the pastor. "You say
we could lose our lives for this child. I would consider
that the greatest honor that could come to my family."[3]

In one account we have a young teenage boy; in the
other a trained and experienced Christian leader. Now which
of these was the good neighbor? Which followed the law
of love? Which one makes the Christian faith compellingly
attractive? Which one is forgettable (along with his faith)?
Which one ought we to follow in our times of trouble no
matter how unpopular or costly?

Chapter 5

Clarifying Right and Wrong in a Relative World

Moral relativism is bankrupt, but critics of the pro-life view insist on playing the tolerance trick. Don't fall for it.

Now we turn to the most common challenge you'll face as a pro-life student. In fact, this challenge is so serious that it can silence your pro-life witness with just five words: "Who are you to judge?"

In his song "Can I Live?" rap artist Nick Cannon tells the story of his own mother who, at age seventeen, was slated to abort him but changed her mind at the last minute. Reflecting on his mother's decision, Nick wrote lyrics as if he were talking to her from the womb, pleading for his life. Here's the line that got him in trouble with some critics: "[Mommy] hopefully you'll make the right decision, and don't go through with the knife incision." Critics were angry—not because Nick's gruesome depiction of abortion was inaccurate (no one challenged that), but because he claimed to be right on a question of morality. They said things like "Who are you to judge?" and "You shouldn't force your personal moral views on others."

Nick Cannon's critics espoused a worldview known as moral relativism. Relativism, in its most basic form, says there are no objective moral standards, only personal preferences. It pretends to be tolerant, neutral, and nonjudgmental, but it's none of those things. Take a look at Nick's critics. When they said he shouldn't judge, they were judging him! And when they said that he shouldn't force his views on others, well, they were forcing that view on him! Nevertheless, relativism, more than anything else, is used to silence pro-life Christians in the name of tolerance. It's a trick. Don't fall for it.

It's all relative!

In their book *Relativism: Feet Firmly Planted in Mid-Air*, Francis J. Beckwith and Gregory Koukl identify three major types of relativism.[1]

1. Society-Does Relativism claims that because cultures disagree on important moral issues, objective moral truths either do not exist or, even if they do exist, we cannot know them. For example, some cultures say it's wrong to have more than one wife while others teach you can have many. Which view is right? The absence of consensus, so the argument goes, means an absence of truth! Yet how does it follow that because people disagree, nobody is right? People once disagreed on slavery—did that mean nobody was correct? Society-does relativism is descriptive, not prescriptive. That is, it only describes what cultures do, not what they ought to do.

2. Society-Says Relativism claims that each society determines right and wrong for itself. What's right for one society may not be right for another. Morality is reduced to a social contract and is determined by popular consensus. But if this is true, there can be no such thing as an immoral society or an immoral law. If a particular society chooses to enslave women or practice racial genocide, who are we, as outsiders, to judge? Indeed, the Nazis used this very defense at the Nuremberg Trials, claiming they had merely followed orders within the framework of their own legal system, one that varied from outside nations. Moreover, if society is the final measure of morality, then all of its judgments are moral by definition. Those who oppose its judgments—for example, moral reformers like Martin Luther King, Jr., and Gandhi—are evil by definition. Society cannot be improved, only changed.

3. I-Say Relativism reduces morality to the individual. I determine right and wrong for myself, meaning no one has a right to judge me. The common expression "Who are you to force your morals on me?" is an example of I-say relativism. Here's the problem: If I-say relativism is true, there can be no immoral individuals, only personal differences.

As a pro-life student, you'll encounter both street-level relativism and its academic cousin on campus. You must equip yourself to engage both.

Street-level relativism

Instead of refuting pro-life arguments, some abortion-choice advocates try to silence them with appeals to relativism. At first glance, relativism seems tolerant and reasonable, but a closer look reveals its flaws.

1. Relativism is self-defeating—that is, it can't live with its own rules. Notice the language used by University of Maryland student Greg Dickinson, who wrote to the campus paper about a pro-life display depicting abortion:

After seeing the gruesome display on Hornbake Mall, I was once again reminded why I am pro-choice. Abortion is a horrible act that should only be reserved for when the health of the mother is in danger or when the circumstances of impregnation were brutal. However, to me this argument is brushed aside. As a gay student who grew up in a conservative area, I know firsthand what it is like to be judged, harassed, humiliated and denied the basic rights to marry the one I love and have a family. These are rights that I feel are *universal*, but conservative moralists have denied me of them. This is why I have developed an unwavering, uncompromising belief that personal morals *must* be kept personal, because no matter how strong my personal beliefs are, I would never have my moral convictions pressed upon another person. Our entire society is built on choice, and it is this freedom of choice that *must* be respected and preserved.[2] (Emphasis added)

Mr. Dickinson claims that morality is personal, but then emphatically states that personal morals must be kept personal (by everyone) and freedom of choice must be respected (by everyone). Question: Says who? Is that his view? If so, who is he to push his personal views onto pro-lifers who disagree? Remember: The person who says "you shouldn't judge" just judged you. The person who claims that you shouldn't force your views on others just forced that view on you.

Moreover, when Jesus condemned judging, he wasn't at all implying that we should never make judgments about anyone. After all, a few verses later, Jesus himself calls certain people "pigs" and "dogs" and "wolves in sheep's clothing" (Matthew 7:6, 15). What Jesus condemns is a critical and judgmental spirit, an unholy sense of moral superiority.

Jesus commanded us to examine ourselves first for the problems we see so easily in others. However, it doesn't follow from this that we should never make judgments. First, Christ instructs us to make proper judgments. "Do not judge by appearances, but judge with right judgment" (John 7:24). Second, Jesus demands that we render even a judgment about him. "Who do you say that I am?" (Mark 8:29).

2. Relativism can't say why anything is truly wrong, including intolerance. If morals are relative to culture or the individual, there is no ethical difference between Adolph Hitler and Mother Teresa; they just had different preferences. The latter liked to help people, while the former liked to kill them. Who are we to judge? But such a view is counterintuitive. We know there's a difference between starving a child and feeding him. Greg Koukl writes: "Relativists find themselves in the unenviable position of having to admit that there is no such thing as evil, justice, fairness, and no obligation of tolerance."[3]

3. Relativists inevitably make moral judgments. If the relativist thinks it's wrong to judge, how can he say that pro-lifers are mistaken in the first place? Isn't he just pushing his socially conditioned view on me? Whenever a relativist says you shouldn't force your views on others, the first words out of your mouth should be "why not?" Any answer given will be an example of him forcing his views on you. As C. S. Lewis points out in *Mere Christianity*, a person who claims there is no objective morality will complain if you break a promise or cut in line.[4]

Relativists are often blind to their own intolerance. Once while driving my sons to a baseball game at Dodger Stadium, a young woman in a white pickup truck began tailgating me. Visibly angered by my pro-life bumper stickers which read "We Can Do Better than Abortion" and "Some Choices Are

Wrong," she stayed on my tail for a mile or so. Finally, she pulled beside me and extended a certain part of her anatomy skyward to convey her feelings. She then cut in front of me.

When I saw her bumper sticker, I couldn't stop laughing. It said (no joke), "Celebrate Diversity." In other words, in a pluralistic society, we should tolerate the diverse views of others. Ironically, she saw no contradiction between her unwillingness to tolerate (or celebrate) my point of view and her bumper sticker that said we should tolerate all points of view. That is what I mean when I say relativists can't help making moral judgments.

Academic relativism: a debate case study

In our October 2009 debate at the University of North Carolina, Nadine Strossen, former resident of the ACLU (1991–2008), defended her case for elective abortion with an appeal to relativism. To summarize her case, reproductive freedom means the freedom to choose whether or not to have children. Laws restricting abortion unjustly curtail that freedom and impose the religious beliefs of some on others who disagree. "Our individual principles of morality cannot control our judicial decisions," she told the audience. "Our obligation is to liberty. We must respect freedom of conscience that allows women a right to choose."

Citing *Roe v. Wade*, Strossen insisted the state should not enter the private realm of family life. Government must remain neutral. She concluded by quoting the Supreme Court's famous "mystery passage" in the 1992 *Casey* decision. "At the heart of liberty is the right to define one's own concept of existence, of meaning, of the universe, and of the mystery of human life."[5]

Setting aside for the moment that each of her above claims assumed the unborn were not human—for example, would she make this same pitch for personal choice and freedom if the topic were killing toddlers instead of fetuses?—her appeal to relativism was seriously flawed in at least three ways.

1. Nadine's appeal to state neutrality is not neutral. Indeed, state neutrality is impossible on abortion. The law either recognizes the unborn as valuable human beings and thus protects them or it does not and permits killing them. By agreeing that human embryos are fitting subjects for abortion, the federal courts are taking a public policy position that the unborn do not deserve the same protections owed toddlers or other human beings. This is hardly a neutral position; it's an extremely controversial one with deep metaphysical underpinnings. Why, then, is it okay for Nadine to legislate her own view on the status of human embryos but not okay for pro-lifers to legislate theirs?

2. Nadine's appeal to moral neutrality also is not neutral. Notice what she says. "Our individual principles of morality cannot control judicial decisions. Our obligation is to liberty and we must respect freedom of conscience." Really? Is that morally true or just her individual principle of morality? It's like she's saying morality is personal, but here are some objective rules everyone must follow—"We must respect freedom. We must respect conscience. We have an obligation to liberty." Says who? Notice she seeks to impose, through law, her own controversial view of morality on pro-lifers who disagree. That is, she smuggles morality into her claim through the back door. Let me be clear. I have no problem with grounding our laws on objective moral principles. Indeed, if we don't, law is reduced to mere power. However, what I do take issue with are those who pretend they are neutral regarding morality and the law. No they are not. Nadine wants to legislate her position every bit as

much as I want to legislate mine. There is no neutral ground here. Everyone takes a position. And I am fully prepared to accept Nadine's position on abortion if she can demonstrate the unborn are not human. But a faulty appeal to neutrality just won't do the trick.

3. Nadine's appeal to relativism provides an insecure foundation for basic human rights. As noted above, she cites the infamous "mystery passage" in *Casey* to argue that liberty means "the right to define one's own concept of existence, of meaning, of the universe, and of the mystery of human life." That is, human nature is not fixed, but determined subjectively. But if that is true, there can be no fixed rights that arise from that nature, including a fixed right to an abortion. So why can't a future Court just arbitrarily decide that women don't have a right to an abortion? The Court didn't say.

At its core, the abortion debate is not only about forcing one's view or judging others. It's about the much larger question of human equality. That is, do all humans have an equal right to life by virtue of their humanity or do only some have it because the Supreme Court says so? Relativists should be careful how they answer. Remember, our founders taught that your fundamental rights flow from your human nature. Yet not one of those rights is secure if power rests with nine men and women to simply define you out of existence. The pro-life side has a better answer that's grounded in an objective truth: We all have an equal right to life because we share a common human nature, and you have that nature from the moment you begin to exist.

Chapter 6

Converting Your Heritage into Your Legacy

We don't make movies about those who tolerate injustice. We make them about death-defying rescuers. Now it's your turn to demonstrate the moral courage required to change the world.

Andre Trocmé lived in German-occupied France during World War II. The story of his life and leadership is told in a book, *Lest Innocent Blood Be Shed: The Story of the Village of Le Chambon and How Goodness Happened There*.[1] In 1987, the movie *Weapons of the Spirit* portrayed how, and at what cost, this village, "with a population of about three thousand impoverished people, saved the lives of about five thousand Jewish refugees. Most of them were children."[2]

They don't write books and make movies about people who make peace with the unjust deaths of others. They write them about people who muster their moral courage and fight for the weak and the innocent, even at their own peril. Andre Trocmé is such a person. He taught, "There are no important divisions between human beings. The main distinction among people is between those who believe that those in need are as precious as they themselves are, and those who do not believe this."[3] He believed God and therefore answered the call to defend the weak and the innocent.

What you face today is not new; it's just your turn. Beginning with the biblical record, you can read the long and resplendent record of people who loved God more than their own lives and so waged a war of love against all things that destroy body and soul.

Reuben rescued Joseph from being killed by his own brothers (Genesis 37:21–22). The Hebrew midwives "feared God" and defied Pharaoh's gendercide policy and rescued their baby boys (Exodus 1:17). The soldiers of Saul rescued Jonathan from murder (1 Samuel 14:45). Obadiah rescued one hundred prophets from Jezebel and provided food and shelter for them (1 Kings 18:4). Esther risked her life to save her people from a royal (legalized) call for genocide (Esther 4:14; 7:3–4).

Christianity from its very beginning has waged a fierce and steady battle against the ancient and unrelenting practices of paganism: abortion, infanticide, exposure, and abandonment.

The world into which Christianity was seeded saw nothing wrong with these crimes against children. In Rome, babies were abandoned outside the city walls to die from exposure or become food for wild beasts. Abortifacient concoctions, using herbs, pessaries, and poisons are well documented in Greek, Persian, Chinese, Arab, and Egyptian cultures. Infanticide was ritualized among Canaanite peoples; they burned babies in pyres as offerings to Molech.

Historian George Grant writes that not only were these forms of child killing common in the time of Christ, but all the intellectuals of the day saw nothing wrong with it. "None of the great minds of the ancient world, from Plato and Aristotle to Livy and Cicero, from Herodotus and Thucydides to Plutarch and Euripides, disparaged child-killing in any way. In fact, most of them actually recommended it."[4]

Then Christ came into the world. And the same Spirit that led him to endure the cross in obedient love and raised him from the dead, filled the hearts of his followers. Immediately, these Christians started to challenge the powers of death with the gospel of life.

Evidence for this arises in the very first generations of Christians. The Didache is one of the earliest documents we have from the Christian community. It was written about the same time (or soon after) that the book of Revelation was written, around the end of the first century, or early in the second. Among its many instructions is a call to cherish and defend innocent human life:

> There are two different ways: the way of life and the way of death, and the difference between these two ways is great. Therefore, do not murder a child by abortion or kill a newborn infant.[5]

Clement of Alexandria (150–c. 215), Tertullian (c. 160–c. 220), Hippolytus (170–235)—early and leading voices of the church as it spread during the first three centuries—all condemned abortion and defended unborn human life. Hippolytus pointed to Mary and Elizabeth and how John leapt for joy in the presence of the just conceived Son of God, just as we have done in this book. He bemoaned the ongoing practice, writing, "Women . . . gird themselves round, so to expel what was being conceived."[6]

With the rise of the Christian empire in the fourth century, church fathers such as Bishop Ambrose (c. 337–397), Chrysostom (347–407), and Jerome (c. 347–420) continued to speak in defense of life. Augustine (354–430) exposed the moral responsibility that men bear in abortion. "They provoke women to such extravagant methods as to use poisonous drugs to secure barrenness; or else, if unsuccessful in this, to murder the unborn child."[7]

Basil of Caesarea (329–379), the great patriarchal hero of the Greek Orthodox wing of the church, was appalled to discover abortionists working in his city. He marshaled the resources of the Christian community and summoned them to lifesaving action. Some years later, the Emperor Valentinian, in response to Basil's work and leadership, criminalized child killing through abortion, infanticide, exposure, and abandonment. In A.D. 374, he declared, "All parents must support their children conceived; those who brutalize or abandon them should be subject to the full penalty prescribed by law."[8] This was a historic moment.

> For the first time in human history, abortion, infanticide, exposure, and abandonment were made illegitimate . . . The exposure walls were destroyed. And the high places were brought low. When Basil died just four years later, at the age of fifty, he had not only made his mark on the church, he had also altered the course of human history.[9]

But as Christian fervor wanes, these practices reemerge. By the sixth century, a new push to end abortion arose and in response, Emperor Justinian (483–565) enacted pro-adoption legislation.

> Should exposure occur, the finder of the child is to see that he is baptized and that he is treated with Chris-

tian care and compassion. They may be adopted as even as we ourselves have been adopted into the kingdom of grace.[10]

Besides the comparison to marriage, adoption is the most prominent point of comparison used to describe the very glory of the gospel itself! Paul wrote, "Blessed be the God and Father of our Lord Jesus Christ who . . . predestined us for adoption through Jesus Christ" (Ephesians 1:3, 5). The gospel is all about adoption. Christianity has always promoted it and practiced it.

During the so-called Middle Ages, from the fifth to the fifteenth centuries, the church added the Feast of the Holy Innocents to its liturgical calendar. Matthew 2:16 tells of Herod's anger over the birth of Christ. Hoping to eliminate this threat to his kingdom, Herod ordered the slaughter of all the boys in Bethlehem and the surrounding area, who were two years old or younger. The wrenching grief of their mothers had been prophesied: "Rachael weeping for her children" and refusing to be comforted, "because they are no more" (Matthew 2:18; see Jeremiah 31:15).

The Feast of the Holy Innocents created an annual point of remembrance for these mothers and provided a teaching point to remind God's people again and again to oppose every form of child killing in their midst.

Today, in both liturgical and nonliturgical churches, there is a growing practice of designating the third Sunday in January as Sanctity of Human Life Sunday. The date was chosen in solemn recognition that on January 22, 1973, the U.S. Supreme Court ruled that the unborn child was not a human being and could be aborted for any reason or no reason. Churches of every denomination are using this annual occasion to proclaim the message of life and support pregnancy help centers, maternity homes, and other good works.

What about during the Reformation era? John Calvin (1509–1564) was the leader of the Swiss Reformation. He called on the church to be as diligent and devoted to the preservation of the innocent as they were to the proclamation of the gospel. He called God's people to suffer for both, if need be.

> Whether in declaring God's truth against Satan's falsehoods or in taking up the protection of the good and innocent against the wrongs of the wicked, we must undergo the offenses and hatred of the world, which may imperil either our life, our fortunes or our honor.[11]

Ignatius Loyola (1491–1556) was one of the most prominent leaders of the Catholic Counter-Reformation. He also called upon his generation of Christians to understand the injustice of abortion and the call of God. Proverbs 24:11 calls us to "Rescue those who are being taken away to death; hold back those who are stumbling to the slaughter." Loyola captures the spirit of this call.

> Life is God's most precious gift. Abortion . . . is not merely an awful tyranny, it is a smear against the integrity of God as well. Suffer as we must, even die if need be, such rebellion against heaven must not be free to run its terrible courses.[12]

One hundred years later, in Paris, the Pastor Vincent de Paul led his church to demonstrate their commitment to holding each life precious by launching special ministries to help galley slaves, abandoned elderly, unwanted children, and convicts. In 1652, de Paul learned of a guild of abortionists operating in the slums of Paris. He took to his pulpit:

Whene'er God's people gather, there is life in the midst of them—yea, Christ's gift to us as a people is life, and that more abundantly. To protect the least of these, our brethren is not merely facultative, it is exigent. In addition though, it is among the greatest and most satisfying of our sundry stewardships.[13]

Two hundred years later, we can read of William Carey (1761–1834). Carey is famous for his creed: "Expect great things from God, attempt great things for God."

Vishal and Ruth Mangalwadi, in their book *The Legacy of William Carey*, outline the remarkable contributions he made to modern India.[14]

As a botanist, Carey published the first books on natural history in India to stress that "all thy works praise thee, O Lord." As an economist, he hated usury. Seeing interest rates from 36 to 72 percent, Carey introduced the idea of savings banks into India. As a businessman, he brought the modern science of printing and publishing to India. As a publisher he printed newspapers, because "Above all forms of truth and faith, Christianity seeks free discussion." As an educator, he started dozens of schools for Indian children of all castes and founded Serampore College.

Above all, Carey was a missionary. His desire was to bring the gospel to the people. He translated the whole Bible into Bengali, Sanskrit, and Marathi. But the same gospel that led him to do all this never allowed him to be silent when innocent blood was being shed. When he moved to Serampore, he discovered that more than one hundred babies were "sacrificed" every year, thrown into the Ganges River, where they were eaten by alligators. "This was looked upon as a most holy sacrifice giving the Mother Ganges the fruit of their bodies for the sons of their souls."[15]

Carey launched an all-out effort to stop this ritual of child sacrifice. He was accused of imposing his moral values on others. Yet this practice was eventually outlawed. And the pro-life legislation that was eventually passed is to this very day called Carey's Edict.

You should be proud of all these people. They are part of your Christian heritage. And we could go on and on. In India, Christians like James Pegg (1793–1850) documented and exposed sati (or suttee), a form of self-immolation pressed upon Hindu widows that forced them to burn themselves to death on their husbands' funeral pyres. In Africa, Mary Slessor worked to end the ritual killing of twins. In Hawaii, Jozef De Veuster (1840–1889), more popularly known as Father Damian, succumbed to leprosy even as he cared for these outcasts. In England, William Wilberforce devoted his career to end the inhumanity of the slave trade.

This is your heritage! What will be your legacy? If you, the second generation of this current pro-life effort, now take up the fight for life, and advance our cause, then it's possible that your children or grandchildren will look back on abortion the way we currently look back on slavery. If you answer this call, you will do well to remember the words of William Wilberforce:

> Never, never will we desist till we . . . extinguish every trace of this bloody traffic, of which our posterity, looking back to the history of these enlightened times, will scarce believe that it has been suffered to exist so long a disgrace and dishonor to this country.[16]

Chapter 7

Keeping Cool under Fire

Next time you're on the hot seat, ask a good question. Before you know it, you'll be back in the driver's seat.

Have you ever been on the hot seat? Think back to your last conversation on abortion. Was it civil or did your friend morph into a human machine gun, firing assertion after assertion your way so you barely got a word in edgewise? Maybe you quit in frustration. Who can blame you?

As Christians, we're called to give a persuasive yet gracious defense for our beliefs (1 Peter 3:15–16). Thankfully, doing that doesn't require that you memorize an encyclopedia of pro-life answers to every objection hurled your way. You just need to ask three simple questions that can make a world of difference in your next conversation. Gregory Koukl calls them "Columbo Questions," named after the famous TV detective played by actor Peter Falk.[1]

At first glance, Columbo doesn't impress. His wardrobe needs a definite upgrade and eloquence isn't his strong suit.

He comes across bumbling, inept, and completely harmless. The crooks are sure he's too dumb to figure things out. They don't realize he is dumb like a fox. He just keeps asking questions and building a case—until he nails them!

The "Columbo" tactic can be used to:

- gain information and keep you out of the hot seat

- reverse the burden of proof

- indirectly exploit a weakness or a flaw in someone's views

There's nothing dirty or tricky about it. Truth is, many pro-life Christians assume the burden of proof when they shouldn't. For example, if I claim there's a pink elephant hanging over your left shoulder (some of you just looked), it's not up to you to refute me; it's on me to prove my claim. Remember this basic rule: Whoever makes the claim bears the burden of proof. I made the claim about the pink elephant so I bear the burden of proof.

Next time you're in a tight spot, get back in the driver's seat by asking the three Columbo questions:[2]

1. What do you mean by that?

This is a clarification inquiry that tells you what your opponent thinks so you don't misrepresent his view. At the same time, it forces him to think more clearly about his own statements. Your tone should be mild and inquisitive. Consider the following claims and note the Columbo question that's in parenthesis:

"The Bible's been changed many times." (Oh? How so?)

"Pro-lifers force their views on others." (In what ways?)

"Embryos are just a mass of cells." (What does that mean?)

"Religious people shouldn't bring their beliefs to the public square." (Do you mean that only nonreligious people should be allowed to participate in government?)

"Abortion is a fundamental right." (What do you mean by fundamental? And where does that right come from?)

Again, the purpose is to gather information and challenge your critic to think more carefully about his view. This last question alone often disarms the challenge.

2. How did you come to that conclusion?

This is the most important Columbo question, and it can be asked a number of different ways. Why do you believe that? How do you know that? What are your reasons for thinking you're right? In each case, you're reversing the burden of proof and putting it back on the person making the claim—where it belongs:

"The Bible is full of fairy tales." (Why would you believe a thing like that?)

"Thousands of women died from illegal abortions." (How do you know that?)

"Fetuses are not self-aware." (Why does one have to be self-aware to have a right to life?

"No one can say which beliefs are right or wrong." (Then why should we believe you?)

"No single religion or person can see the whole truth. Each sees only a part." (How could you possibly know that each sees only a part unless you can see the whole, something you just claimed was impossible?)

"How did you come to that conclusion?" reverses the burden of proof and gets you out of the hot seat. It forces critics to give reasons for their claims.

3. Have you considered the implications of your view?

Here you are gently demonstrating that your critic pays too high a price for his view. It's critically important that your tone remain gracious. Otherwise, your opponent will become defensive.

"Everything is just an illusion." (Have you considered that if that's true, we could never know it?)

"Fetuses have no right to life because they are not self-aware." (Have you considered that newborns aren't self-aware either?)

"You shouldn't judge people!" (Have you considered that you just did?)

Putting it all together

Your Philosophy 101 professor just told the class that human embryos can be killed for medical research because they lack a conscious desire to go on living. You decide to politely engage him using the three Columbo questions:

You: Dr. Fenton, when you speak of having a "desire," do you mean one that I'm consciously aware of?

Dr. Fenton: Yes, that's exactly what I mean.

You: Thank you for clarifying that. Could you explain why I must have a conscious desire for something before I can justly lay claim to it? In other words, why are conscious desires value giving in the first place?

Dr. Fenton: It seems to me that if I don't consciously desire something, I'm not really harmed if you prevent me from having it. Embryos have no conscious desires for anything, including life, so they're not harmed if we use them for research.

You: Have you considered that a slave can be conditioned not to desire his freedom, yet he's still entitled to it in virtue of his humanity? And what if my desire to live is greater than yours? Does that mean I have a greater right to life than you?

A week later, Dr. Fenton tosses another provocative claim in your direction. "The Christian Bible is silent on abortion. Nowhere between its covers will you find the command 'thou shalt not abort.'"

Once again, you engage him with Columbo questions:

You: What do you mean when you say the Bible is "silent"? Do you mean the word is not mentioned, or that we can't draw any conclusions from what's written?

Dr. Fenton: Both, really.

You: Just to be clear, are you saying that whatever the Bible doesn't expressly condemn, it condones?

Dr. Fenton: I'm just saying the word *abortion* doesn't appear anywhere, and that points toward its permissibility.

You: What are your reasons for thinking their alleged silence justifies abortion?

Dr. Fenton: If the biblical authors don't see fit to mention abortion—let alone condemn it—why not let people draw their own conclusions?

You: Have you considered that the Bible doesn't condemn many things by name including female infanticide and drive-by shootings?

Whenever possible, engage with questions.

In one-on-one or small group discussions, you're better off engaging listeners with questions before stating your own position. For example, if you're told the law can't stop all abortions, you should ask:

Do you mean "all" or do you mean "most"?

How do you know that most women won't obey the law?

Have you considered that laws against rape don't stop all rape, but they do drastically reduce its frequency? Why would it be any different with abortion?

Again, the goal is to engage your critics, not silence them. Stop worrying about winning a debate. Just keep asking good questions. "Christians should get out of the habit of trying to refute every fantasy a nonbeliever imagines or every claim he manufactures out of thin air," writes Greg Koukl. "Don't take up the defense when the other person is the one making the claim. Why let him off so easily?"[3]

So the next time you hear that embryos are just clumps of cells, don't run for cover. Step up and ask, "Why would you believe a thing like that?"

Next thing you know, you'll be back in the driver's seat.

Chapter 8

Winning with Winsomeness

The aroma of life is attractive. Don't stink up the room!

My coauthor, Scott, travels around this country and publicly debates the staunchest proponents of legal abortion. You will never hear Scott demean the person he is debating. You will watch him expose the logical fallacies in their position. You may see him expose the emotional red herrings sometimes used to mask the radical nature of their commitment to legal abortion without limits. But you will not see Scott use ridicule or call them names or say or do anything that smacks of a personal attack against the people he debates. He has devoted his life to defeating the legitimacy of abortion. But he will not so much as roll his eyes at his opponents.[1] Why is that?

Part of the answer involves consistency. How we argue, in words and tone, ought to match the human dignity that we are arguing for. Part of the answer is maturity. Scott has come to genuinely care for his opponents. Part of the answer is also practical. The people we seek to win over are influenced, for good or ill, by how we behave as much as by what we believe. Winning means being winsome, as well as being right.

It's true that the likability of the messenger does not determine the truthfulness of a message. But it does factor in to how a message is received. The people who spend millions of dollars to sell you stuff know this well. They spend a great deal of time making sure that the message bearer is likable. Marshall McLuhan's famous axiom, "the medium is the message," originally pointed out how the medium of communication (TV versus radio versus a letter, etc.) influences the message and the reception of the message. But the axiom is just as much used today to remind people that what we say and how we say it are connected and directly affect receptivity. This, of course, is not new.

"With patience a ruler may be persuaded, and a soft tongue will break a bone" (Proverbs 25:15). That's power! "A soft answer turns away wrath, but a harsh word stirs up anger" (Proverbs 15:1). There's power even in politeness. Proverbs 15:4 says that "a gentle tongue is a tree of life." For a people calling people to life, that is well worth remembering.

There is power, too, in a hot temper or rash words, but of another sort. As Proverbs 12:18 says, "There is one whose rash words are like sword thrusts, but the tongue of the wise brings healing." And again, "The tongue of the wise commends knowledge, but the mouths of fools pour out folly" (Proverbs 15:2).

Always remember, speaking with respect and being patient wins great favor with people. It opens their heart to listen. It does not, by itself, carry the day. But dismissive tones can lose the day before your case has even been heard. And the damage is lasting. People remember it and project it onto the next person who engages in the case for life. The aroma of life is attractive. Don't stink up the room!

The Bible's most basic communications rule is "speak the truth in love" (Ephesians 4:15). That is sublime. You will always do well following this guideline. Ask "what is true?" and you will resist the fear that pressures you to conform to what pleases others and gains their approval. Question. Test. Examine. Think. Search for truth like a pirate searches for treasure. Love truth. Die for truth, if need be.

At the same time, ask yourself, "Am I leading with love?" Truth without love is like a hard rain. The water runs right off. Truth with love is more like a steady rain that soaks in. Love is a conquering power. When people see that you care for them as a person, it's nearly impossible for them not to listen to you more. Speak the truth in love.

Consider how these two worked together to win over the most famous pro-abortion advocate in the world: Norma McCorvey, a.k.a. Jane Roe, the plaintiff in the infamous Supreme Court case *Roe v. Wade*, that declared state laws against abortion unconstitutional. She writes, "Abortion was the sun around which my life orbited. I once told a reporter, 'This issue is the only thing I live for. I live, eat, breathe, think everything about abortion.'"[2]

When we disagree with others, we invariably believe the worst of them. Confrontation over legal child killing is inevitable. Just our honest description of it is offensive to the sensibilities of our opponents, even if we say it without malice or condemnation.

Norma continues:

I called Flip Benham, the brash and bold leader of Operation Rescue, Flip "Venom." Flip called me "responsible for the deaths of 35 million children." We were supposed to be sworn enemies, but due to the persistence of a local real estate agent, we became next door neighbors whose offices shared a common wall.[3]

An inevitable clash of values emerged as the staff of the abortion business would meet the pro-life demonstrators. Norma writes:

> Occasionally, the clashes would collapse into conversation. During one friendly banter, I goaded Flip, "What you need is to go to a good Beach Boys concert." Flip answered, "Miss Norma, I haven't been to a Beach Boys concert since 1976." The seemingly innocuous response shook me to the core. All at once, Flip became human to me.[4]

Engaging Norma this way sent a strong message: the difference between them was not personal! Flip signaled friendship, and it rocked her world. And to this he added patience and, I suspect, earnest prayers. This love was sorely tested. Norma continues:

> During one abortion day confrontation, I charged up to Anne Hollacher, an O.R. volunteer who was holding a picket sign, . . . I called Anne every name I could think of, which was usually enough to make the toughest protesters wilt, but Anne maintained her composure. When I saw that Anne wouldn't budge, I spit in her face. Anne smiled. I was furious. "How dare you look at me like that?" I screamed. "How dare you smile at me?" Anne politely wiped the spit off her face with her sleeve. "Jesus loves you and so do I," she said. "And I forgive you." [5]

Love shakes people to the core. You begin to question your long-held beliefs. Then the lie, soaked with love, like a hillside slowly softens and then gives way. In a moment your whole worldview is mud.

In Norma's case, her defense of abortion gave way soon after she put her faith in Christ.

When my conversion became public knowledge, I spoke openly to reporters about still supporting legalized abortion in the first trimester. The media was quick to use this to downplay the seriousness of my conversion, saying I typified the "general ambivalence" of our culture over abortion. But a few weeks after my conversion, I was sitting in O.R.'s offices when I noticed a fetal development poster.

The progression was so obvious, the eyes were so sweet. It hurt my heart, just looking at them. I ran outside and finally, it dawned on me. "Norma," I said to myself, "They're right." I had worked with pregnant women for years. I had been through three pregnancies and deliveries myself. I should have known. Yet something in that poster made me lose my breath. I kept seeing the picture of that tiny, 10-week-old embryo, and I said to myself, that's a baby! It's as if blinders just fell off my eyes and I suddenly understood the truth—that's a baby!

I felt crushed under the truth of this realization. I had to face up to the awful reality. Abortion wasn't about "products of conception." It wasn't about "missed periods." It was about children being killed in their mother's wombs. All those years I was wrong. Signing that affidavit, I was wrong. Working in an abortion clinic, I was wrong. No more of this first trimester, second trimester, third trimester stuff. Abortion—at any point—was wrong. It was so clear. Painfully clear.[6]

Norma's conversion was painful and her personal struggles over her past continue. But take note of the title of her story. She called it *Won by Love*.[7] When the history of this moral struggle is written, one of the most stunning developments will be how many of the people who started, led, or worked in the abortion industry were won over to the cause of life—and more, to the cause of Christ.[8]

There is something powerfully winsome about a position held with such confidence that patience, kindness, and grace emanate from it. It opens the heart and allows the mind to weigh challenging ideas. If you signal that you care and you help people think, they will come to the life position more often than not. So witness to the truth. And demonstrate love.

Chapter 9

Rape and Abortion

How should we treat innocent human beings that remind us of a painful event? That one question gets to the heart of the matter.

Whenever possible, I take questions from the audience after my talks. I don't need to guess what the first one will be because it's nearly always the same.

"Okay, say a woman is raped. If she gives birth, the child will remind her of the rape—forever! Do you think abortion is wrong in that case?"

Two types of people ask about rape and abortion, the learner and the crusader. The learner is genuinely trying to work through the issue and resolve it rationally. The crusader just wants to make you, the pro-lifer, look bad. In either case, it's our job to demonstrate wisdom and sensitivity. I begin with the following:

"That's an important question and you are absolutely right. It would be foolish to ignore her pain or minimize the trauma she experienced and its long-term effects. Even if her attacker is punished to the fullest extent of the law—which he should be—her road to recovery will be tough."

Then, very delicately, I continue by asking one primary question, then a follow-up:

"Given we both agree the child may provoke unpleasant memories, how do you think a civil society should treat innocent human beings that remind us of a painful event?" (Pause and let the question sink in.) "Is it okay to kill them so we can feel better?"

Listener: Well, no, I guess not.

Me: And why is that?

Listener: Because they are human?

Me: That's right. So if the unborn are human beings, how do you think we should treat them when they remind us of something painful?

Listener: Hmmm. I don't know.

Me: Think of it this way. Suppose I have a two-year-old up here with me. His father is a rapist and his mother is on antidepressant drugs. At least once a day, the sight of the child sends her back into depression. Would it be okay to kill the toddler if doing so makes the mother feel better?

Listener: No.

Me: And that's because he's a human being?

Listener: Yes.

That first question—"How should we treat innocent human beings that remind us of a painful event?"—gets to the crux of the issue that must be resolved: What is the unborn? Only after clarifying the primary issue do I make my case:

Me: Here's the point I'm getting at. If the unborn are human, killing them so others can feel better is wrong. Hardship doesn't justify homicide. Admittedly, I don't like the way my answer feels because I know the mother may suffer consequences for doing the right thing. But sometimes the right thing to do isn't the easy thing to do.

Listener: These are hard things to think about.

Me: I agree. Here's one more example that may help. Suppose I'm an American commander and terrorists capture my unit. My captors inform me that in ten minutes, they'll begin torturing me and my men to get intelligence information out of us. However, they are willing to make me an offer. If I will help them torture and interrogate my own men, they won't torture and interrogate me. I'll get by with no pain. Can I take that deal? There's no way. I'll suffer evil rather than inflict it. Again, I don't like how the answer feels, but it's the right one. Thankfully, the woman who is raped does not need to suffer alone. Pro-life pregnancy help centers are standing by to help get her through this. We should help, too.

What I've said so far usually satisfies the learner. She may still feel uncomfortable thinking about the rape victim suffering for doing good, but she's begun to grasp the moral logic that's in play.

The crusader, on the other hand, will hear none of it. He's out to score debate points. He appeals to the hard case of rape, but his appeal is flawed because it's not entirely truthful.

Here's why. The abortion-choice position he defends is not that abortion should be legal only when a woman is raped, but that abortion is a fundamental right she can exercise for any reason she wants during all nine months of pregnancy. Instead of defending this position with facts and arguments, he disguises it with an emotional appeal to rape. But this will not make his case. The argument from rape, if successful at all, would only justify abortion in cases of sexual assault, not for any reason the woman deems fit. In fact, arguing for abortion-on-demand from the hard case of rape is like trying to argue for the elimination of all traffic laws because a person might have to break one rushing a loved one to the hospital.[1] Proving an exception does not prove a rule.

To expose his smoke screen, I ask a question: "Okay, I'm going to grant for the sake of discussion that we keep abortion legal in cases of rape. Will you join me in supporting legal restrictions on abortions done for socioeconomic reasons which, as studies on your side of the issue show, make up the overwhelming percentage of abortions?"[2]

The answer is almost always no, to which I reply, "Then why did you bring rape up except to mislead us into thinking you support abortion only in the hard cases?"

Again, if the abortion-choice crusader thinks that abortion should be a legal choice for all nine months of pregnancy for any reason whatsoever, including sex-selection and convenience, he should defend that view directly with facts and arguments. Exploiting the tragedy of rape victims is intellectually dishonest. But even worse, it degrades the very women it pretends to care about by using their own personal tragedy as a cover up for abortion-on-demand.

Pro-life advocates aren't cruel when they insist that one human should not be killed to make another feel better. They're simply refocusing the debate on the one question we can't ignore: What is the unborn?

Chapter 10

Listening to the Victims of Sexual Assault

Compassion means to "suffer with" others. So bear their anguish, don't add to it by coming up with a solution that makes you feel better, but not them.

It is doubtful than any of your fellow students have thought carefully about rape and recovery. Rape elicits such justifiable horror that we react rather than think. We can only guess at how to be loving and caring. But listen to a real victim, Kathleen DeZeeuw:

> I, having lived through rape, and having raised a child "conceived in rape," feel personally assaulted and insulted every time I hear that abortion should be legal for rape and incest. I feel that we're being used to further the abortion issue, even though we've not been asked to tell our side of the story.[1]

What is Kathleen's side of the story? What does she think is a compassionate and just response to sexual assault and pregnancy? Researcher Dr. David Reardon has been studying cases of sexual assault resulting in pregnancy for many years. In his book, *Victims and Victors: Speaking Out about Their Pregnancies, Abortions and Children Resulting from Sexual Assault*, Reardon interviewed nearly 200 women like Kathleen. He writes:

> Typically, people on both sides of the abortion debate accept the premise that most women who become pregnant through sexual assault want abortions. From this "fact," it naturally follows that the reason women want abortions in these cases is because it will help them to put the assault behind them, recover more quickly, and avoid the additional trauma of giving birth to a "rapist's child."[2]

Most people, including sexual assault victims who have never been pregnant, project what is best, and we end up hurting these victims even further if we are not careful.

My own bias was revealed by how stunned I was to learn that about 75 percent of victims of sexual assault resulting in pregnancy do not have abortions. They give life, parent, or place for adoption.[3]

Why? First, many women who become pregnant through sexual violence recognize that abortion still kills an innocent human being—in this case their own child. Asking "what is it?" clarifies the issue is spite of the pain. Evidently most women, pregnant as a result of rape, sense that their own well-being and that of their own child are never at odds. They see what their quick-to-advise friends fail to see: they are not made whole by killing their own progeny. They live or die together.

Reardon writes, "Many of the women in our sample aborted only because they were pressured to do so, and most reported that the abortion only increased their experience of grief and trauma." One such victim wrote:

> I soon discovered that the aftermath of my abortion continued a long time after the memory of my rape had faded. I felt empty and horrible. Nobody told me about the pain I would feel deep within causing nightmares and deep depressions. They had all told me that after the abortion I could continue my life as if nothing had happened.[4]

In contrast, none of the women Reardon interviewed who carried to term, reported that she regretted giving birth or wished that she had chosen abortion instead. Remarkably, and no doubt a testimony to the human spirit, these women said that their children had brought peace and healing to their lives. How is that possible?

By giving birth, victims of rape fight back. They return good for evil and in doing so regain their lost dignity. Reardon concludes:

> Giving birth, especially when conception was not desired, is a totally selfless act, a generous act, a display of courage, strength, and honor. It is proof that she is better than the rapist. While he was selfish, she can be generous. While he destroyed, she can nurture.[5]

Since this is how the victims see things, we ought to help them rather than make ourselves feel good by making the problem go away (as if recovery from rape were as simple as getting rid of the evidence).

In addition, these women often see the hand of God at work in their pregnancy. They sense that their child is the one good thing to come out of a horrible, repulsive act. And they sense purpose and meaning in the life of their child. This too ought to be respected and supported.[6]

If you serve in a pregnancy help center, as I have for the past twenty years, you will eventually see this very dynamic unfold. Martha Avila, who directs Heartbeat of Miami, recently sent me the following account:

Lici came from Cuba at 14 and worked on her English using the internet. She met a "friend" online. Not having much experience, she didn't see anything wrong because he was just one of her "schoolmates." Lici agreed to meet him after school one day. He invited her to drive around in his car. Olga, Lici's mother, was desperate waiting for Lici to get home. And her worst fears were realized. Lici was raped by this "schoolmate" who turned out to be a 27-year-old man. Afterward, he threatened to kill Lici's mother if she told anyone.

Several weeks later, Olga seeing that something was wrong, brought Lici to our Pregnancy Help Medical Clinic. Lici had been crying a lot. Her mother did not understand what had happened, but suspected that her daughter was pregnant.

If so, Olga was determined to save her daughter's future by demanding that Lici have an abortion. "She is too young to be having sex. She won't tell me who her boyfriend is. She can't have a baby!" Yesenia, the pregnancy help counselor, watching Lici react to her mother, sensed something more troubling was going on. She took Lici in to speak to her privately and the whole terrifying truth came out. Yesenia assured Lici that no harm would come to her mother and that it was safe to tell her mother what happened. Afterwards they called the police. Thank God this evil predator is behind bars now and will never strike again.

But what about the baby? The ultrasound revealed a beautiful eight-week-old baby. Lici cried, pleading for the life of her child. All she could say was, "It is not my baby's fault. No matter how it happened, this baby is inside of me and I am the mom."

Yesenia shared God's love with Olga and Lici. She told them how God works for good for those who trust him, even out of evil. They then discussed adoption. Lici courageously told her mother that she would rather place her baby in the arms of adoptive parents than to kill her baby.[7]

Martha included a picture of Lici and her baby, born January 1, 2011. Was it difficult? No words can describe it. But Lici and her whole family found the genuine compassion of the Christian community to be both lifesaving and life-changing.

Abortion is inherently unhealthy to womanhood and motherhood. I've concluded that women suffer abortions the way they suffer car accidents, as a traumatic experience with a long recovery process. Remarkably, women who have suffered the trauma of rape and then pregnancy more often than not realize that abortion only adds to the trauma and meets the needs of those around them, more than their own needs. If you want to be boldly compassionate, listen and learn from those who have "been there." Be ready to stand with victims of rape and help them give life and return to life.

Chapter 11

What about Back-Alley Abortions?

> *Every death from abortion is a tragedy we all should mourn, but why should the law be faulted for making it more risky for one human to intentionally take the life of another completely innocent one?*

The coat-hanger argument is no more persuasive now than it was forty years ago. But don't think for a moment that it's going away anytime soon.

The summer of 2005 is a case in point. As soon as Justice Sandra Day O'Connor announced her retirement from the Supreme Court, abortion-advocacy groups were all over the media insisting that women would die by the thousands if President Bush appointed a pro-life justice to replace her. The National Organization for Women played the fear card for everything it was worth. The group told parents that if *Roe v. Wade* was overturned, their daughters might very well number among the dead.[1]

More recently, Kris Hamel of DANFORR (Detroit Action Network for Reproductive Rights) claimed that prior to *Roe v. Wade*, "an estimated 5000 to 10,000 women died each year in the United States as a result of a million unsafe, illegal abortions."[2]

The alleged argument has strong emotional appeal. We're told that if abortion is restricted or regulated in any way, women will be forced into the back alleys of America where they will die from rusty coat-hanger abortions. Who wants that? And given the law can't stop all abortions, why not keep the practice legal?

That's the argument. Here's what's wrong with it.

First, it begs the question. That is, unless you begin with the assumption that the unborn are not human, you are making the highly questionable claim that because some people will die attempting to kill others, the state should make it safe and legal for them to do so.[3] Why should the law be faulted for making it tougher for one human being to take the life of another, completely innocent one? Should we legalize bank robbery so it's safer for felons? As abortion-advocate and philosopher Mary Anne Warren points out, "The fact that restricting access to abortion has tragic side effects does not, in itself, show that the restrictions are unjustified, since murder is wrong regardless of the consequences of prohibiting it."[4] Again, the issue isn't safety. The issue is the status of the unborn.

Bottom line: If you think a particular argument begs the question regarding the status of the unborn, simply ask if this justification for abortion also works as a justification for killing toddlers or other humans. If not, the argument assumes the unborn are not fully human. Again, it may be argued that the unborn are not fully human and abortion is therefore justified. But this must be argued with evidence, not merely assumed by one's rhetoric.

Second, the objection that the law cannot stop all abortions is silly. Laws cannot stop all rape; should we legalize the practice? The fact is that laws against abortion, like laws against rape, drastically reduce its occurrence. In their sophisticated statistical analysis, Barbara Syska, Thomas Hilgers, and Dennis O'Hare argue that prior to *Roe v. Wade* (1973), there were at most two hundred ten thousand illegal abortions per year while more conservative estimates suggest an average of eighty-nine thousand per year.[5] Within eight years of legalization, abortion totals jumped to more than 1.3 million annually![6] True, no law can stop all illegal behavior, but that's not the point. At issue is the status of the unborn: Are they human beings? If so, we should legally protect them the way we would any other group that is unjustly harmed.

Third, women aren't forced to have illegal abortions; they choose to have them. Yes, pro-lifers mourn the loss of any woman who dies needlessly, but I refuse to accept the premise that women must seek illegal abortions. Greg Koukl writes, "A woman is no more forced into the back alley when abortion is outlawed than a young man is forced to rob banks because the state won't put him on welfare. Both have other options."[7]

Finally, the claim that thousands died annually from back-alley abortions prior to 1973—when *Roe. v. Wade* legalized abortion in the U.S.—is just plain false. Dr. Mary Calderone, former medical director for Planned Parenthood, wrote in 1960 that illegal abortions were performed safely by physicians in good standing in their communities. True, this doesn't prove no woman will ever die from an illegal abortion, but it does put to rest NOW's claim of high mortality rates for the years prior to legalization. Here's Calderone's quote in context:

Fact No. 3—Abortion is no longer a dangerous procedure. This applies not just to therapeutic abortions as performed in hospitals but also to so-called illegal abortions as done by physicians. In 1957, there were only 260 deaths in the whole country attributed to abortions of any kind. In New York City in 1921 there were 144 abortion deaths, in 1951 there were only 15; and, while the abortion death rate was going down so strikingly in that thirty-year period, we know what happened to the population and the birth rate. Two corollary factors must be mentioned here: first, chemotherapy and antibiotics have come in, benefiting all surgical procedures as well as abortion. Second, and even more important, the conference estimated that 90 percent of all illegal abortions are presently being done by physicians. Call them what you will, abortionists or anything else, they are still physicians, trained as such; and many of them are in good standing in their communities. They must do a pretty good job if the death rate is as low as it is. Whatever trouble arises usually comes after self-induced abortions, which comprise approximately 8 percent, or with the very small percentage that go to some kind of non-medical abortionist. Another corollary fact: physicians of impeccable standing are referring their patients for these illegal abortions to the colleagues whom they know are willing to perform them, or they are sending their patients to certain sources outside of this country where abortion is performed under excellent medical conditions. The acceptance of these facts was such that one outstanding gynecologist at the conference declared: "From the ethical standpoint, I see no difference between recommending an abortion and performing it. The moral responsibility is equal." So remember fact number three: abortion, whether therapeutic or illegal, is in the main no longer dangerous, because it is being done well by physicians.[8]

In addition, the Centers for Disease Control report that thirty-nine women died from illegal abortions in 1972, the year prior to legalization, not five to ten thousand as claimed by abortion advocates for each year prior to *Roe*.[9] Admittedly, the thirty-nine deaths are understated, but as abortion-choice ethicist Daniel Callahan points out, the claim of five to ten thousand deaths per year is simply out of the question. Callahan's own survey of available data suggests a more accurate figure of five hundred deaths annually.[10] Yes, each of those deaths is tragic. We shouldn't minimize a single one. However, legalizing abortion isn't the solution. "The true response to back-alley abortions," writes Stephen Schwarz, "is to be outraged at all abortions, to condemn all abortions—not to propose one kind (legal) in place of another (illegal)."

In short, the coat-hanger appeal is not really an argument, but a veiled threat: "Give us choice or else! Only then will abortion be safe."

Question is, safe for whom?

But suppose the mother truly isn't safe. What then? We turn to that question next.

Chapter 12

What about Abortion to Save the Mother's Life?

While it's always wrong to intentionally take the life of an innocent human being, it's not wrong to save one life rather than lose two.

Pro-life advocates do not say that it's always wrong to take human life—a position only a strict pacifist would hold. Rather, we say it's always wrong to intentionally kill innocent human beings, and we believe elective abortion does just that.

But what if the mother's life is in danger due to the pregnancy? If saving her life means that her unborn child will die, is that intentional killing?

To be clear, the vast majority of abortions worldwide are not medically necessary to save the mother's physical life. As reported in the journal *International Family Planning Perspectives*, most are done to delay giving birth or for socioeconomic concerns that include "disruption of education or employment; lack of support from the father; desire to provide schooling for existing children; and poverty, unemployment or inability to afford additional children."[1]

Dr. Warren Hern, whose 1990 book *Abortion Practice* is the standard medical teaching text on late-term abortion, agrees that the majority of abortions "are sought for socioeconomic reasons." These decisions to abort, he writes, "are usually made on the basis of such factors as desire or lack of desire for parenthood, stability of relationships, educational status, emotional status, or economic status, among others."[2]

Suppose, however, the pregnancy does in fact pose a grave threat to the mother's life. What is the morally correct way to proceed?

Ectopic pregnancy (EP) is a clear case in point. With EP, the developing human embryo implants somewhere other than the uterus, usually on the inner wall of the fallopian tube. This is an extremely dangerous situation for the mother. When the EP outgrows the limits of the narrow fallopian tube enclosing it, the tube bursts resulting in massive internal hemorrhaging. In fact, EP is the leading cause of pregnancy-related death during the first trimester.[3] The accepted medical protocols in this case are to end the pregnancy through chemical (Methotrexate) or surgical intervention, with surgery being the superior treatment of choice.[4] There is no way the developing human can survive EP. If the mother dies from internal bleeding, the embryo dies also, given he's too young to survive on his own. At the same time, the limits of current medical technology do not allow transfer to a more suitable environment. Despite out best intentions, we simply can't save the child.

What is the greatest moral good we can achieve in this situation? Is it best to do nothing and let two humans (likely) die, or is it best to act in such a way that we save one life even though the unintended and unavoidable consequence of acting is the death of the human embryo?

Pro-life advocates almost universally agree we should do the latter. As Christopher Kaczor points out, "the fact that a medical procedure brings about fetal death with certainty does not mean that it is intentional or direct abortion."[5] For example, suppose the pregnant mother has a cancerous uterus and will die if it's not surgically removed. Nearly all ethicists agree she may have the surgery even though her unborn offspring dies when her uterus is removed. However, while her child's death was foreseen in the act of saving the mother, that death was not intended.

Ectopic pregnancy can be seen the same way. Given the situation, it's better to save one life than lose two. Notice once again, however, the intent of the physician is not to intentionally kill the developing human, but to save the mother's life. The unintended and unavoidable consequence of that lifesaving act is the death of the embryo. Perhaps in the future we can plant the embryo to a more desirable location. If that day comes, we should do that. But for now, if we do not act, both mother and child die. It's best that one should live.[6]

Some pro-lifers object to Methotrexate (MXT) as a treatment for EP on grounds that it's intentional killing, whereas surgical removal of the embryo may not be. The use of MXT, so the argument goes, acts directly on the body of the embryo and invariably leads to its death.

However, it doesn't follow that because you act directly on the body of another person—even in a manner that guarantees his death—that you intended to kill him. Kaczor points to an example from Theophile Raynaud (1582–1663), where an innocent man is fleeing unjust attackers on horseback. To his horror, the man discovers a child on a narrow bridge that he must cross or be overtaken by his aggressors. Can he continue his flight even though the child will certainly be killed? In his flight, writes Kaczor, the horseman acts directly on the child in a way that brings lethal harm, but he does not intend that harm. The lethal consequence is a side effect of the action and is foreseen rather than intended.[7]

As for other alleged threats to the mother's life, few are truly life threatening. Most can be managed with proper physician oversight. Dr. Thomas Murphy Goodwin oversees a large high-risk pregnancy clinic in Los Angeles that averages between fifteen thousand and sixteen thousand births annually. Excluding cases diagnosed late in pregnancy, only one or two cases a year pose an immediate lethal threat to the mother's life.[8] Goodwin writes that even women suffering from cancer can be treated with chemotherapy and the fetus tolerates the treatment.

Chapter 13

Cross Bearing for the Child Bearing

*All women considering abortion
do so for compelling reasons.
Rescuing means freely and
sacrificially taking up their problems
and making them your own.*

When students discuss the life issue, they raise the exceptional cases of rape, incest, and the life of the mother as possible justifying circumstances for abortion. But the women and couples who turn to abortion every day (about 3,300 in the United States and Canada alone) have their own personal and circumstantial reasons for doing so. These people see them as compelling and justifiable in their own right. If you are going to provide these women and couples with a life-affirming alternative, you must understand them and their real needs. Start by setting aside your own understanding.

Students for life think philosophically and ethically about abortion. You make categories and run things through the grist mill of hierarchical values. But your fellow students and co-workers, who are in the grip of a pregnancy crisis, do not process things so neatly.

When conversing with those in crises, it's a mistake to think that your goal is merely apologetic in nature—that if we educate them to see the humanity of their unborn child that the consequent moral imperative "abortion is wrong" will always follow. It doesn't.

The truth is, most women who succumb to abortion don't believe in abortion! Students for life are often shocked to learn this. They ask me, "If they believe it's wrong, how can they do it?" I reply, "Have you never done something that you knew was wrong?" I once stole a hat. I did not lack knowledge. I lacked self-control. I lacked the ability to resist temptation. I lacked faith in God to provide for my needs. I lacked contentment in what he had provided. I knew fully well that stealing was wrong. That's why I was trying to be sneaky about it! People do things contrary to their conscience all the time.

I have counseled thousands of women in the past twenty years who were considering abortion and tens of thousands more through the staff and volunteers serving at the nine pregnancy help centers I have helped establish. The majority of these women feel a need to say, "I know it's wrong." Then they justify it. Due to their difficult personal circumstances, they have "no choice." What they were saying is not true. They do have choices. But it feels true.

A sixteen-year-old girl called me once. A few minutes into our conversation, she said, "If I don't get an abortion, I'm going to kill myself." There was a pause, then she whispered words I will never forget. "After I have my abortion, I know I'm going to kill myself."

That was a crystalizing moment for me. I finally understood the death grip that many, and probably most, women experience when they discover that they are pregnant and are unprepared for it. Her pregnancy felt like a sentence of death. Remember this! Some women have described the feeling of desperation as akin to "an animal chewing off its leg to get out of a trap." Abortion looks like a desperate but necessary way to save one's own life. It isn't true in a medical sense, but it feels true psychologically. This is what my sixteen-year-old friend was expressing.

On the other hand, she was sensitive to the life within her. She was sensitive to the terrible truth—that she was about to kill her own baby. Since a large part of her self-image was that she was the kind of person who would never hurt a child, she understood that she was about to do something so violent and contrary to her own beliefs and values, that she would not be able to live with herself afterward.

Most of your fellow students, who find themselves pregnant, feel this death grip. They have a vision for their lives. Like you, they have clear goals and plans of where they will be in a few years and what they will be doing. Often this is a shared vision with parents, who are investing a lot of money in their education as a stepping stone to something else. This is the life that is now threatened; their life as they project it. In this sense, the pregnancy is a life-threatening condition.

Some fascinating right-brain–left-brain research was done in the late nineties on how women who are pregnant process their options. What they found was shocking to the ordinary pro-lifer. Paul Swope explained:

> Unplanned motherhood represents a threat so great to modern women that it is perceived as equivalent to a "death of self." While the woman may rationally understand this is not her own literal death, her emotional,

subconscious reaction to carrying the child to term is that her life will be "over." This is because many young women of today have developed a self-identity that simply does not include being a mother. It may include going through college, getting a degree, obtaining a good job, even getting married someday; but the sudden intrusion of motherhood is perceived as a complete loss of control over their present and future selves. It shatters their sense of who they are and will become, and thereby paralyzes their ability to think more rationally or realistically.

When these women evaluate the abortion decision, therefore, they do not, as a pro-lifer might, formulate the problem with the radically distinct options of either "I must endure an embarrassing pregnancy" or "I must destroy the life of an innocent child." Instead, their perception of the choice is either "my life is over" or "the life of this new child is over." Given this perspective, the choice of abortion becomes one of self-preservation, a much more defensible position, both to the woman deciding to abort and to those supporting her decision.

When a woman faces an unplanned pregnancy, her main question is not "Is this a baby?"—with the assumed consequence that if she knows it to be so she will choose life. Women know, though often at the subconscious level, that the fetus is human, and that it will be killed by abortion. But that is the price a woman in that situation is willing to pay in her desperate struggle for what she believes to be her very survival. Her central, perhaps subconscious, question is rather, "How can I preserve my own life?"[1]

How to be a lifesaver

To be a lifesaver, you must do what lifesavers do every day in pregnancy help centers.

You must give her hope. Help her envision her life beyond the crises. Help her see that her life plans may be delayed, but that they will not be destroyed by having a baby.

You must give her truth. You must help her see and understand how having an abortion will change her life as much as by having a baby, but in different ways.

You must amplify the voice of her own moral conscience. She will express moral ambivalence, but this voice is smothered under the shouting voices of fear. You must help her see how following rather than compromising her own beliefs and values, no matter the difficulties, makes her a better person and a stronger one.

Let me illustrate. A young man came to my local pregnancy help center to arrange for an abortion for his girlfriend. He told me they had no choice but to have an abortion. Usually when the girlfriend is not present, I know there is some ambivalence at work. I asked him, "Tell me why having a baby seems impossible to you right now." He ticked off several reasons right away: "We are not married and her parents will be very angry and ashamed if they find out she is pregnant now. I don't make enough money right now to support a baby. We are planning on getting married in the spring, but by then she would be showing. Too embarrassing!"

I replied that this was all very understandable but that before they made a final decision, they ought to also consider how the abortion might also impact their lives together. We walked through a list of the common health risks associated with abortion.

Breast Cancer: The risk of breast cancer almost doubles after one abortion, and rises even further with two or more abortions.

Cervical Cancer: Women who have had one abortion face a 2.3 relative risk of cervical cancer, compared to women who have never had an abortion.

Placenta Previa: Abortion increases the risk of placenta previa in later pregnancies (a life-threatening condition for both the mother and her wanted pregnancy).

Immediate Complications: Approximately 10 percent of women undergoing elective abortion will suffer immediate complications of which approximately one-fifth (2 percent) are considered life-threatening.[2]

We looked at a fetal model and I helped him understand fetal development. But even then, my focus was to help him grasp why abortion so often leads to depression, guilt, blame, and bitterness in women after an abortion, and how that affects their relationship.[3] The man looked over the risks and grew concerned. He turned to me and asked, "Do you think it might be okay if we just went ahead and had this baby?"

I said, "Perhaps. But what about her parents?"

He said, "I need to go talk to them myself. It's my fault. I pressured her. I need to apologize and take the heat on this."

I said, "Okay, but what about the money situation? You can't afford a baby!"

He replied, "I can get a second job."

I said, "Okay, but the wedding! She will look pregnant!"

He dismissed me. "We can just move the wedding date up a bit."

He walked in seeing the baby as a threat to all his plans. He left with a vision for providing and protecting his family. He later returned with his girlfriend to have me go over everything again with her.[4]

Let me illustrate how you can help women and couples hear the voice of their own conscience and how you can amplify it. After I listen and learn their circumstances and express my understanding of why that might be considering abortion, I ask, "What do you understand about abortion? How did you feel about abortion before you found yourself in this current situation?" Most will express some ambivalence.

"I don't like it."

Ask, "Why don't you like it?"

"I know it's wrong."

Ask, "Why is it wrong?"

They may continue with more nonanswer answers.

"It's against my religion."

Ask, "Why is your religion against abortion?"

"It's killing."

Ask, "It's killing what?"

"It's killing . . . you know . . . a baby."

Finally, the voice of their own conscience has spoken plainly, and their own ears have heard it from their own lips. Then restate and amplify it.

"In other words, you are telling me that in spite of all your difficult circumstances, you understand and believe that if you proceed with your abortion, that you are killing your own baby."

"Yes."

"Then don't do it. You will never be the same."

At this point, I show them pictures, beautiful ones of unborn babies. I give them a fetal model. I explain, "This is why you believe abortion is wrong. Abortion is an act of violence that kills a baby." On occasion, I show pictures of abortion at this point—to show them why they don't like abortion.

As that door of escape slams shut, I immediately start opening other doors. I offer them my personal help. "Let's look at some alternatives and see if together, we can't help you make a decision you can live with."

One final example is needed. Scott always says that when making the case for life, "Bring out the toddler!" That is also helpful when women or couples considering abortion say, "I don't really believe in abortion, but I have no choice." This is a lie. Break it, and you save the baby.

A couple came to see me. They had nine children. The oldest was fifteen years old. His wife was fifteen weeks pregnant. She did not speak English and so just watched and listened. She was downcast and sullen. The husband was in a panic.

"I don't really believe in abortion, but I have no choice. I cannot afford ten children."

I expressed amazement at their big family and how wonderful their children looked. I sympathized with his predicament. "I can understand why you're thinking about abortion." Then I trotted out the toddler, only in this case, it was actually the fifteen-year-old.

I said, "If money is the main issue, then I think I have your solution."

"What's that?" he asked.

"I would kill the fifteen-year-old. You'll save more money."

He looked at me a moment and translated my advice to his wife. They had a lively conversation at that point that I was not privy to, then he turned back to me and said, "We can't do that!"

Then I explained that he had ten children right now and the question before him is, which one will he kill in order to save the most money? He got it.

The point is that when people say that they don't believe in abortion, they believe this in a vague way, but not in a concrete way. They don't honestly see the unborn child as human as their toddlers (or their teens). Until you help them grasp the moral equivalence, the baby is in danger. Once they do, they will treat their unborn child as their other children.

"We just can't kill our children to save money," I told him. "There must be a better way." He whispered this to his wife. In addition, I pledged to help him find more resources for his beautiful family. His wife wept openly with relief.

Women and couples who turn from the brink of abortion, hold fast to their faith and their values, and work toward a life-affirming alternative generally come to look back on this time of their life, not with shame, but as their finest hour. Your mission, should you accept it, is to walk them back from the brink and bring them to this better place.

Cross Bearing for the Child Bearing

However, count the cost! Sometimes a simple word is all it takes. But usually lifesaving work is strenuous work. Jesus was forthright about the demands of love in pointing to the time-consuming and personal sacrifices required of the Samaritan to save one life. When you step up to help a mother in crisis, you are taking up her problems and making them your own. You are cross bearing for the child bearing!

My friend Fern, who counsels at a pregnancy help center, befriended a pregnant college student Dawn (not her real name). Fern set out many urgent prayer requests as she

struggled to save Dawn and her baby from abortion. Collectively these petitions created a diary of sorts.

Aug. 3: Dawn made an appointment for Thursday to get
an abortion and while she feels terrible about it, she also
feels like she has no choice. Pray that her heart is changed!

Aug. 10: She is twelve weeks along but missed her appointment. She had some good conversations with people
at the pregnancy center. She is now considering adoption.

Aug. 13: Things are down again. She now has an abortion scheduled for Monday. Pray!

Aug. 17: Missed appointment again! God is working in
her life.

Sept. 1: We've hit another rocky period. She has an abortion scheduled for tomorrow. She found out today that her
parents are planning a trip to visit her and she is panicking.

Sept. 15: Missed third appointment. But feels like she
has no choice. Please pray today.

Sept. 20: She fears her parents but has agreed to another ultrasound (a breakthrough).

Sept. 22: I was with her for her ultrasound. She saw
her baby moving and made the realization that she wants
to carry her baby. Please keep praying against attack by the
enemy. We are overwhelmed by seeing God's hand move in
this situation and are so very thankful for the prayers lifted
up by each one of you. God is good!!

Want to end abortion? Then prepare yourself. Deepen
and strengthen your love for God. Your strength to love will
grow. Then God will lead you to someone in crisis. Then, with
faith toward God, take up their burdens and help them find
God's provision for life.

Chapter 14

What about the Mantra "My Body, My Choice"?

?

Does a mother have no more duty to her own child than she does a stranger who is unnaturally hooked up to her?

Most arguments for elective abortion simply assume the unborn are not human beings. The bodily rights argument is an exception. Its central claim is that a pregnant mother has a right to bodily autonomy that trumps the right to life of the child she carries. Judith Jarvis Thomson first raised the bodily rights issue in a 1971 essay titled "A Defense of Abortion."[1] In her essay, Thomson bites the bullet: She concedes for the sake of argument the humanity of the unborn. However, she contends that no woman should be forced to use her body to sustain the life of another human being. Just as you may refuse to support a neighbor with the use of your kidney should his fail, so, too, a woman may refuse the use of her body to support the developing human. Thomson then presents a thought experiment:

> You wake up in the morning and find yourself back to back in bed with an unconscious violinist, a famous unconscious violinist. He has been found to have a fatal kidney ailment, and the Society of Music Lovers has canvassed all available medical records and found that you alone have the right blood type to help. They have therefore kidnapped you, and last night the violinist's circulatory system was plugged into yours, so that your kidneys can be used to extract poisons from his blood as well as your own. The director of the hospital now tells you, "Look, we're sorry the Society of Music Lovers did this to you—we would never have permitted it if we had known. But still, they did it, and the violinist now is plugged into you. To unplug you would be to kill him. But never mind, it's only for nine months. By then, he will have recovered from his ailment, and can safely be unplugged from you." Is it morally incumbent on you to accede to this situation? No doubt it would be nice of you if you did, a great kindness. But do you have to accede to it?

There's no mistaking Thomson's claim: Just as one may withhold support and detach himself from the violinist, so, too, the mother may withhold support and detach herself from the child. Abortion is such a detachment.

Do the Parallels Work?

Thomson wants us to believe that pregnancy is similar to the mother being hooked up to the violinist. But are they truly similar in morally relevant ways? If so, Thomson's case seems virtually unassailable. If not, the analogy fails and her argument crumbles. There are good reasons to reject Thomson's alleged parallels.

First, we may not have the obligation to sustain strangers who are unnaturally plugged into us, but we do have a duty to sustain our own offspring. As Stephen Schwarz points out, the very thing that makes it plausible for Thomson to say that you have no duty to sustain the violinist—namely, that he's a stranger unnaturally hooked up to you—"is precisely what is absent in the case of the mother and her child."[2] Gregory Koukl asks, "What if the mother woke to find herself surgically connected to her own child? What kind of mother would willingly cut the life-support system to her two-year-old in a situation like that? And what would we think of her if she did?"[3] In short, Thomson assumes a mother has no more duty to her own offspring than she does a total stranger who is naturally hooked up to her.

Second, the child is not an intruder. He is precisely where he naturally belongs at that point in his development. If the child doesn't belong in the mother's womb, where does he belong? "That a woman looks upon her child as a burglar or an intruder is already an evil, even if she refrains from killing her," writes Schwarz.[4]

Third, Thomson tries to justify abortion as merely the withholding of support. But it's more—the killing of a child through dismemberment, poison, or crushing. Thomson may (we assume) withhold support from the violinist; she may not actively kill him. "Assume that the woman has no duty to sustain the child," writes Schwarz. "This means only that she has the right to withhold her support from him. It does not give her the right to kill the child—which is what abortion is. Thomson seizes on the withholding of support aspect of abortion, suppressing the deliberate killing aspect."[5] That the woman throws the child out in the name of withholding support does not mean that she does not also do something else—kill the child.

As Francis J. Beckwith points out, "Euphemistically calling abortion the 'withholding of support' makes about as much sense as calling suffocating someone with a pillow the withdrawing of oxygen."[6] If the only way I can exercise my right to withhold support is to kill another human being, I may not do it.

Fourth, barring cases of rape, a woman cannot claim that she bears no responsibility for the pregnancy in the same way she bears no responsibility for the violinist. Merely going to bed at night does not naturally cause anyone to wake up attached to a total stranger. However, when a couple engages in sexual intercourse, they engage in the only possible activity that naturally leads to the formation of a child. Hence, she is not like the woman who finds herself plugged into the violinist against her own will.

No Limits Allowed

During our debate at U.C. Davis in June 2006, Dr. Meredith Williams, who performs some abortions, more or less claimed that women have an absolute right to bodily autonomy. However, during the cross-examination, she backed off that claim when I pressed her with this thought experiment from Dr. Rich Poupard:

Let's say a woman has intractable nausea and vomiting and insists on taking thalidomide to help her symptoms. After having explained the horrific risks of birth defects that have arisen due to this medication, she still insists on taking it based on the fact that the fetus has no right to her body anyway. After being refused thalidomide from her physician, she acquires some and takes it, resulting in her child developing no arms. Do you believe that she did anything wrong? Would you excuse her actions based on her right to bodily autonomy? The fetus after all is an uninvited guest, and has no right even to life, let alone an environment free from pathogens.[7]

When Dr. Williams said the woman was wrong to do that, I replied: "So if the mother harms her unborn child with thalidomide, that's wrong, but if she kills it with elective abortion, that's fine? But who are you to say that? If the mother's right to bodily autonomy is absolute, it's none of our business what she does with the fetus, right?" Like it or not, abortion-choice advocates must live with the consequences of their view. If bodily autonomy reigns supreme, no limits on abortion are acceptable. Period. Dr. Williams can't have it both ways.

Consider a final example. In 2004, Melissa Rowland was prosecuted for refusing an emergency Caesarian section to save the lives of her unborn twins. According to the hospital staff, Rowland refused the C-section because of the scar it would leave on her body. She stated she preferred to "lose one of the babies than be cut like that." Nevertheless, emergency room doctors and nurses repeatedly tried to persuade Rowland to have the C-section, but she insisted on going outside for a smoke instead. She finally yielded to their demands, but by then it was too late. One baby died and the other required intense medical intervention to survive. The surviving twin, like his mother, tested positive for cocaine. The medical examiner's report stated that had Rowland consented to the surgery when doctors originally urged her to, the baby would have survived.[8] Rowland was subsequently charged with murder. Kim Gandy of the

National Organization for Women said she was "aghast" that Rowland was criminally charged. She's got a point. If unborn humans have no legitimate claims on their mothers' bodies, why not let a drug-addicted mom wait around for another smoke?

Chapter 15

Revealing the Truth about Abortion

Abortion is beyond words. And at its core, it is a faith issue.

This is the information age. We quickly reach the point when more is less. We can quickly reach our saturation point.

"Yak, yak, yak!"

"Blah-blah, blah blah blah!"

"Yada, yada, yada!"

Too many words, or words used too often, lose their power to convey truth. Abortion is one of those words. It's utterly incapable of conveying the truth to which it points.

This works in favor of the advocates and defenders of legal abortion. They know that when people see a picture of abortion they understand the truth about abortion in a way that speaking about the "abortion issue" actually hides. They know that when pro-lifers replace the empty word *abortion* with more accurate descriptions, that it sounds inflammatory. This breaches the rules of etiquette when discussing an "issue." So the average listener then believes we have inflated our case. We lose credibility and thus we lose them.

What Is It?

What is abortion then? Bernard Nathanson comes the closest I have seen to capturing in words, the reality we are up against. But even here, he is admitting that words fall way short of the truth that is abortion. He says:

> The abortion holocaust is beyond the ordinary discourse of morality and rational condemnation. It is not enough to pronounce it absolutely evil. . . . The abortion tragedy is a new event, severed from connections with traditional presuppositions of history, psychology, politics, and morality. It extends beyond the deliberations of reason, beyond the discernment of moral judgment, beyond meaning itself. . . . This is an evil torn free of its moorings in reason and causality, an ordinary secular corruption raised to unimaginable powers of magnification and limitless extremity.[1]

He speaks this way because he has seen abortion up close and personal.[2] He has seen the truth thousands of times, counting the body parts to make sure he has removed them all. He knows what abortion is. It's an act of violence that kills a baby.

You must be willing to show people this. [See photo on the following page.] Words alone rarely carry the day. I show people the truth of abortion in pictures (or video) to explain why it's proper and accurate to describe it as an act of violence that kills a baby. I show them the pictures to help them understand why I think it's the greatest moral evil of our times.

Fetus aborted 8 weeks after conception

Among all the offenses of man, the greatest offense is shedding innocent blood. In tracing out the breaking point when God moves from patiently warning to active judgment, Scripture says it's the killing of innocent people, or passively accepting the killing of innocent people, that is so offensive to him that it finally invokes his wrath. So we read,

> The Lord sent . . . Chaldeans . . . against Judah to destroy it. . . . Surely this came upon Judah at the command of the Lord, to remove them out of his sight, for the sins of Manasseh, according to all that he had done, and also for the innocent blood that he had shed. For he filled Jerusalem with innocent blood and the Lord would not pardon. (2 Kings 24:2–4).

This also is the message of the prophets. Some prophets brought this message as an indictment—as part of their call to repentance lest judgment come. Other prophets brought this message as a reminder of why judgment already fell on them. In both cases, they pointed to the shedding of innocent blood: "You have become guilty by the blood that you have shed" (Ezekiel 22:4).

Among all the ways that sinful man finds to shed innocent blood, the most offensive to God is child sacrifice. This is the most heinous form because in child sacrifice, God is made part of the atrocity. His name and reputation are brought into the killing as if he would want or demand such a thing. Child sacrifice is something so utterly profane and insulting to a holy and loving God that he himself calls it unthinkable: "They built the high places of Baal in the Valley of the Son of Hinnom, to offer up their sons and daughters to Molech, though I did not command them, nor did it enter into my mind, that they should do this abomination, to cause Judah to sin" (Jeremiah 32:35).

So Israel was taught, "You shall not give any of your children to offer them to Molech, and so profane the name of your God: I am the LORD" (Leviticus 18:21).

So horrifying and offensive is child sacrifice to the sensibilities of a God who loves children and created them for great purpose, that he also warns Israel not to passively accept child sacrifice, but to intervene and stop it.

> And if the people of the land do at all close their eyes to that man when he gives one of his children to Molech, and do not put him to death, then I will set my face against that man and against his clan and will cut them off from among their people, him and all who follow him in whoring after Molech. (Leviticus 20:4–5)

Perhaps the clearest expression of God's outrage against the slaughter of innocent children is found in

Ezekiel 16:20–21. Here child sacrifice is recorded in very personal terms:

> And you took your sons and your daughters, whom you had borne to me, and these you sacrificed to them to be devoured. Were your whorings so small a matter that you slaughtered my children and delivered them up as an offering by fire to them?

God takes the death of every child personally; he takes the slaughter of innocent children as nothing less than the murder of his own children.

Abortion Is Child Sacrifice

Whatever the reasons we cling to in order to justify abortion, they are no match for what the conscience knows and Scripture confirms is "child sacrifice." We want our lives to go according to our plans. The baby is sacrificed to secure them.

Kim Flodin, a staunch defender of abortion rights and a freelance writer, had two abortions. She wrote of her anguishing circumstances and subsequent guilt and injuries for *Newsweek* magazine. She concluded, "I was pregnant, I carried two unborn children and I chose, for completely selfish reasons, to deny them life so that I could better my own."[3] That is the perfect definition of child sacrifice as it unfolds today.

We no longer sacrifice our children to please some pagan, bloodthirsty god like Molech. We have made ourselves into a god and sacrifice our children for our own ends. We abort because of money, believing we cannot afford a child and do the other things we want to do with our money. We abort to save ourselves the embarrassment of others discovering our promiscuity and to save our reputations. We abort to save relationships or educational and vocational goals we have planned. There are many understandable reasons for abortion. But they all share the same DNA; they all sacrifice a child to gain something else.

Abortion Is a Substitute for Prayer

All the stated reasons for abortion, though, are really penultimate reasons. The ultimate reason is spiritual in nature. We abort instead of trusting God to provide for our needs. Or as James 4:2 says, "You desire and do not have, so you murder." This is the spirit of abortion. And why do we not have what we need? James continues, "You do not have, because you do not ask [God]." Abortion, then, is a substitute for prayer.

Abortionists Are Substitute Saviors

Strange and perverse as their end is, abortionists parrot the same message that Christ offers to those in trouble: "Come to me, all who labor and are heavy laden, and I will give you rest. Take my yoke upon you" (Matthew 11:28–29). Like Christ, abortionists promise deliverance. Like Christ, the abortionist promises to save their lives. The only difference is that one sells death as deliverance, and the other gives life.

Your calling, as a lifesaver, is largely one of helping women and couples in pregnancy distress turn to the true Savior for deliverance. Even if you are not speaking directly about spiritual things, when you help a woman choose life, you are helping her believe. What are you helping her believe? That in spite of her difficulties, and even though she cannot see how, God (or Providence) will provide a way for her to feed and care for her child. Abortion is a no-confidence vote in God (or Providence). Choosing life is a statement of faith that somehow, God will provide. To choose life is to learn how to pray, "Give me today, my daily bread."

Perhaps this is why talking openly about spiritual matters is, more often than not, a welcome part of the discussion with women and couples struggling with pregnancy. It's not imposing. It's catching up with their own internal questions. They see how the decision before them is spiritual. They have been praying and crying out to God about what to do. Don't forget this. Abortion is a spiritual crisis as much as a biological one. It forces people to decide what they believe and who they believe in. Help them trust in the true Savior for all their needs.

You have been trained to keep your "spirituality to yourself." Don't believe this, especially when you are talking to somebody in pregnancy crisis. In this context it is good to ask spiritual questions, like, "Tell me what you believe. What does your faith instruct you to do? How are you reconciling this decision with your own belief in God?"

The nature of this struggle is cosmic in scope. It's good versus evil. It's life versus death. Satan comes to devour (Revelation 12:4). Christ comes to deliver. You are called to trust God and get into the fight for life. Ignatius Loyola (1491–1556) said it well:

> Life is God's most precious gift. Abortion . . . is not merely an awful tyranny; it is a smear against the integrity of God as well. Suffer as we must, even die if need be, such rebellion against heaven must not be free to run its terrible courses.[4]

Chapter 16

If Men Can't Get Pregnant, Should They Speak Up on Abortion?

Arguments don't have gender; people do. It's intellectually dishonest to contend otherwise.

Sometimes an argument is so silly, it's best to treat it like a kid.

Think back to when you were ten. In the heat of arguing with your sibling, you had a one-word answer that could stop him in his tracks. Remember what it was?

"So?"

Done right, you could end the argument in two sentences.

"You called me stupid!"

"So?"

It's a word you need to put back in your vocabulary, only this time without the attitude that usually went with it.

For example, suppose you deliver a stellar two-minute defense of the pro-life view in your speech class. You argue from science that from the earliest stages of development, your classmates were distinct, living, and whole human beings. Philosophically, you contend there's no relevant difference between the embryos they once were and the young adults they are today that justifies killing them at that earlier stage of development. Differences of size, level of development, environment, and degree of dependency are not good reasons for saying they could be killed then but not now.

Hands shoot up immediately. First up is long-haired male bearing a huge peace sign on his T-shirt. "Do you also oppose capital punishment? If not, doesn't that make you inconsistent?" Next is an econ student. "Are you willing to adopt and feed all these babies you don't want aborted? If not, who are you to say what's right?" A split second later, the leader of the college Democrats gets a standing ovation with her take: "You're a man. Men don't get pregnant. What gives you the right to even talk about this issue?"

Time to Fight Like a Kid

Each of these objections misses the central question in the abortion debate—namely, is the unborn one of us? You answered that question with your two-minute speech However, instead of answering your pro-life case, your opponents attack your alleged behavior. We call this the ad-hominem fallacy, because even if the personal attacks are true, they do nothing to refute the argument you presented. A childish attack deserves a kidlike response:

"So?"

Suppose the guy with the peace sign is right. You're inconsistent because you oppose abortion but support capital punishment. Now, I don't think that's true, but let's go ahead and grant his point for the sake of discussion. Setting aside for the moment that the sword cuts both ways—that is, he supports abortion but opposes capital punishment, and that makes him inconsistent—how does your alleged inconsistency mean that (1) the unborn are not human, and (2) killing them is justified? Could the unborn still be human even if you're inconsistent? You might reply as follows:

You: Maybe you could clarify this for me. Suppose I'm against capital punishment. What's your next move?

Peace Guy: What do you mean?

You: Does abortion suddenly become wrong if I agree that capital punishment is wrong?

Peace Guy: Well, no.

You: Then what's your point?

In other words, "So?"

The same is true for the adoption attack. How does your alleged unwillingness to adopt a child justify an abortionist killing one? What if I said: "Unless you agree to adopt my three sons by noon tomorrow, I shall execute them!" If you turn down my ultimatum, am I justified carrying out my threat?

Again, "So?"

The "you're a man" objection suffers from similar flaws. First, arguments do not have genders, people do.[1] Suppose a pro-life woman offers the same arguments as a pro-life man. What's the abortion-choice advocate's next move? Does elective abortion suddenly become less permissible? If not, what's the point of attacking the pro-lifer's gender?

Second, the gender sword cuts both ways. If men can't speak on abortion, *Roe v. Wade*, the Supreme Court case legalizing abortion, was bad law. After all, nine men decided it. Abortion-choice advocates should also call for the dismissal of all male lawyers working for Planned Parenthood and the ACLU on abortion-related issues. Since abortion advocates are unwilling to do this, we can restate their argument as follows: "No man can speak on abortion—unless he agrees with us." This is a classic case of intolerance.

Third, since post-menopausal women cannot get pregnant; must they be silent on the issue? Think of the bizarre rules we could derive from this argument: "Since only generals understand battle, only they should discuss the morality of war." Or, "Because female sportscasters have never played in the NFL, they have no right to broadcast *Monday Night Football!*"

Again, abortion advocates must offer facts and arguments to support their position. Attacking people personally, even if those attacks are true, will not make their case or refute ours.

Chapter 17

Manning Up!

Abortion is a men's movement.
Ending it will require mature
and faithful men to man up!

To the immature, self-centered man, who sees his sexuality largely in terms of conquest and recreation, the modern feminist creed "My Body! My Choice!" is a dream come true. It can mean only one thing to him: "Pregnant? Not my problem!" Now spread this notion of liberation to a whole generation of men, and you have a problem. So starting with us, we men need to be part of the solution.

Men Are Part of the Problem

In some surveys, men favor legal abortion at about the same percentage as women.[1] But in many others, men favor legal abortion more than women do[2] A May 2009, Rasmussen poll found women were far more pro-life than men. They found 64 percent of women believe most abortions are morally wrong, a view shared by just 51 percent of men.

One survey reported that men were also more likely to think abortion improved male-female relationships, while the majority of women disagreed. Well, of course they do! Consciously or unconsciously, legal and accessible abortion enables men to be more sexually promiscuous, since it allows for the dreaded complication of a baby to be dealt with. Legalized abortion is a men's liberation movement. Even the dumbest man on the bus, with all the stereotypical passions of football, beer and sex, knows this. But among the radical feminists, only a few highly intellectual leaders have made note of it. Catherine MacKinnon is one of them. She writes:

> Abortion facilitates women's heterosexual availability. In other words, under conditions of gender inequality [abortion] does not liberate women; it frees male sexual aggression. The availability of abortion removes the one remaining legitimized reason that women have had for refusing sex besides the headache. [Roe's] right to privacy looks like an injury got up as a gift, for virtually every ounce of control that women won [from legalized abortion] has gone directly into the hands of men.[3]

That is why the early feminists, such as Susan B. Anthony (1820–1906) and Elizabeth Cady Stanton (1815–1902) ardently opposed abortion. They understood how it provided another avenue for sinful men to exploit women. It allowed them to pressure women into surrendering their babies or simply abandoning them. Ironically it opened the option needed to convince women that they had "no choice." A passage in Anthony's and Stanton's newspaper, *The Revolution*, shows how well they understood this:

Guilty? Yes, no matter what the motive, love of ease, or a desire to save from suffering the unborn innocent, the woman is awfully guilty who commits the deed. It will burden her conscience in life, it will burden her soul in death; but oh, thrice guilty is he who drove her to the desperation which impelled her to the crime![4]

Nothing has changed. After forty years of legal abortion, millions of women can testify how their "right to abortion" turned into an expectation from others. Here is a typical account:

My family would not support my decision to keep the baby. My boyfriend said he would give me no emotional or financial help whatsoever. All the people that mattered told me to abort. When I said I didn't want to, they started listing reasons why I should. That it would have detrimental effects on my career, and my health, and that I would have no social life and no future with men. Could I actually do it alone? I started feeling like maybe I was crazy to want to keep it.

I finally told everyone that I would have the abortion. . . . I was scared to not do it because of how my family and boyfriend felt. I'm so angry at myself for giving in to the pressure of others. I just felt so alone in my feelings to have my baby.[5]

According to Frederica Mathewes-Green in her book *Real Choices*, the highest number of women (38.2 percent) resort to abortion in response to pressure from a husband or a boyfriend.[6] Sociologist Dr. David Reardon, in his book *Aborted Women, Silent No More*, found the same thing. "The opinions and pressures of others played a major role in the final decision of most aborting women . . . nearly 55 percent of the respondents felt they had been very much *forced* to abort by others; 51 percent of the time this other person was a husband or boyfriend."[7]

Dr. Phillip Ney, a Canadian researcher of abortion's psychological effects, reports that in a first pregnancy, if a woman's partner is present but not supportive, she has a four times greater chance of having an abortion; if the partner is absent, she has a six times greater chance of aborting. During a second pregnancy, if the partner is present but unsupportive, there is a 700 percent increased chance of abortion; and if the partner is absent, there is an 1800 percent increased chance of abortion.[8]

Immature, self-centered men are the main reason women succumb to abortion. Mature men carry an innate sense of obligation to provide and protect women and children; especially their own wives and children. Quaint? Perhaps. But women were well served by it. Abortion on the other hand aborts this value in men. Women are the not the stronger for it. As Wendy Shalit observes:

> I was born in 1975, and from anorexia to date-rape, from our utter inability to feel safe on the streets to stories about stalking and stalkers, from teenage girls finding themselves pregnant to women in their late 30's and early 40's finding procreation miserably difficult, this culture has not been kind to women. And it has not been kind at the very moment that it has directed an immense amount of social and political energy to "curing" their problems.[9]

In contrast, Elizabeth Cady Stanton, fighting with all her might for suffrage, condemned abortion as degrading to women. "When we consider that women have been treated as property, it is degrading to women that we should treat our children as property to be disposed of as we see fit."[10]

Again, I am struck at the clarity with which the early feminists saw abortion and the need for change. Sarah Norton, the first woman to argue for coeducation at Cornell University, wrote in 1870:

> Child murderers practice their profession without let or hindrance, and open infant butcheries unquestioned. . . . Is there no remedy for this antenatal murder? . . . Perhaps there will come a day when . . . an unmarried mother will not be despised because of her motherhood . . . and when the right of the unborn to be born will not be denied or interfered with.[11]

Oh! May that day come soon. And brothers, you have a vital role to play!

Men Must Be Part of the Solution

There is a precise, specific, clearly marked, and underscored starting point for every man to begin his pro-life activism. Practice sexual integrity! Since this is a term you may be unfamiliar with, let me say it more plainly. Your first contribution to the cause of life and the ending of abortion is to personally protect the women in your life from being at risk for abortion because you got them pregnant outside of marriage. You do that best by practicing sexual self-control: waiting until marriage and being faithful within marriage.[12]

Walking in integrity means doing right by others in your dealings—not lying or cheating or using people, but acting honestly and justly toward them. The mature and godly person cherishes integrity and its inherent reward.

"Whoever walks in integrity walks securely, but he who makes his ways crooked will be found out" (Proverbs 10:9).

Sexual integrity points to doing things right in matters of the heart.[13] It means "flee[ing] sexual immorality" (1 Corinthians 6:18). For men it means treating women outside of marriage "like sisters, in all purity" (1 Timothy 5:2). For women it means not using sensuality and sexuality as bait, but as the proper expression of intimate marital love.[14] For men and women it means committing yourself to the revealed will of God regarding your sexuality:

> For this is the will of God, your sanctification: that you abstain from sexual immorality; that each one of you know how to control his own body in holiness and honor, not in the passion of lust like the Gentiles who do not know God; that no one transgress and wrong his brother in this matter, because the Lord is an avenger in all these things, as we told you beforehand and solemnly warned you. (1 Thessalonians 4:3–6)

Sexual sins are particularly damaging. They are not private sins. The partner involved is profoundly affected by it. Sexuality binds us emotionally, but since this is sex without covenant, it binds, then rips. It hurts. And there is no condom for the heart! Plus, if your lack of sexual integrity leads to pregnancy, you have now greatly added to the injury.

So brothers, if you want to be pro-life, first do no harm! Take the lead in this matter of sexual integrity. Trust me on this, women welcome it.

Before I close, let me state the obvious. Yes, sexual integrity applies to women as well. Wendy Shalit writes:

> It is always hard to separate what you really want from what you're supposed to want, but try this as a thought

experiment. Women, when no one else is around, do you secretly long for a whole series of men; to arbitrarily marry one of them and then maybe have affairs, maybe not—to be cool and wait and see if anyone better comes along, and then divorce—or do you long for one enduring love? That's a loaded question, but still, if you could be guaranteed that no one would laugh at you, would it be the latter? If yes, why do you allow your culture to shatter your hopes?[15]

Sexual integrity for the Christian man and woman means trusting that what we really desire—a healthy, tender, long-term mutually satisfying relationship—God also desires for us. Only he abbreviates this description to one word: marriage. Then he works in and through us to help us achieve one that fits this very description. That's life! Be radically pro-life!

Chapter 18

Is War Worse than Abortion?

Some moral issues are contingently wrong while others are absolutely wrong. Indeed, to be worse than abortion, how bad would an unjust war have to be?

In 2008, a handful of notable "pro-life" evangelicals and Catholics threw their support behind a presidential candidate sworn to uphold elective abortion as a fundamental right. They argued that doing so constituted an enlightened "pro-life" vote that was morally superior to the narrow party politics of religious conservatives. Instead of passing laws against abortion, so the argument went, the candidate and his party would "reduce" it by addressing its underlying causes.[1] True, he was mistaken on abortion, but he was right on other, important "whole-of-life" issues such as opposition to war, concern for the poor, and care for the environment.[2]

What's really at stake?

Each of these alleged "pro-life" votes represents a profound misunderstanding of the pro-life position. The fundamental issue before us is not merely how to reduce abortion, but who counts as a member of the human family. How we answer will determine whether embryos and fetuses enjoy the protection of law or remain candidates for the dumpster. As Francis Beckwith points out, a society that has fewer abortions but protects the legal killing of unborn humans is still deeply immoral.[3] Given what's at stake, it's vital that pro-life Christians persuasively answer four key questions related to war, social justice, and politics.

1. Why don't pro-lifers oppose war like they do abortion?

War can be a moral evil, but it isn't always so. Careful thinkers make distinctions between intrinsic (absolute) moral evils and contingent ones. For example, the decision to wage war may or may not be wrong, depending on the circumstances. However, the decision to intentionally kill an unborn human being for socioeconomic reasons is an intrinsic evil and laws permitting it are scandalous. True, a general in a just war may foresee that innocent humans will die securing a lasting peace, but he does not intend their deaths. With elective abortion, the death of an innocent human fetus is not merely foreseen; it's intended. Problem is, many Catholics and left-leaning evangelicals are perfectly willing to support a political party that supports an intrinsic evil simply because its members promise to help us avoid contingent ones. This is bad moral thinking.

2. Why are pro-life advocates focused narrowly on abortion when there are other issues?

Of course abortion isn't the only issue—any more than the treatment of slaves wasn't the only issue in the 1860s or the treatment of Jews the only issue in the 1940s. But both were the dominant issues of their day. Thoughtful Christians attribute different importance to different issues, and give greater weight to fundamental moral questions. For example, if a man running for president told us that men had a right to beat their wives, most people would see that as reason enough to reject him, despite his expertise on foreign policy or economic reforms. The foundational principle of our republic is that all humans are equal in their fundamental dignity. What issue could be more important than that? You might as well blame politicians like Winston Churchill and Franklin Roosevelt for focusing too narrowly on defeating the Nazis, to the neglect of other issues. Given a choice, I'd rather pro-lifers focus on at least one great moral issue than waste their precious resources trying to fix all of them.[4]

3. Why don't pro-life advocates care about social justice here and in developing countries?

They do, which is why pro-life pregnancy help centers vastly outnumber abortion clinics in the United States and why committed Christians, most of whom are pro-life, give more than their secular counterparts.[5]

Nevertheless, pro-life Christians should reject the premise that because they oppose the deliberate and unjustified killing of innocent human beings, they must therefore take responsibility for all of the world's ills. Is the American Cancer Society wrong to focus on one deadly disease to the exclusion of others? It's highly unfair to demand that local pro-life groups take their already scarce resources and spread them even thinner fighting every social injustice imaginable. This would be suicide for those opposed to abortion. As the old saying goes, "He who attacks everywhere attacks nowhere."

True, as defenders of human dignity, we should care about the poor, clean water, and the rights of others everywhere. But the U.S. government is not going to solve those problems in developing countries the way it can solve abortion here. For example, our government can't ban poverty or stop the sex trade of young girls in Thailand. That is the job of that nation's citizens and government! However, the U.S. government can and should ban the killing of unborn humans within its own borders. That is why prudent pro-lifers have always sought both moral and political solutions to that problem. While poverty and sex trade are evil, no one in America proposes legalizing them.

Abortion is different. Far from reducing the practice, our government currently advocates it both here and abroad. For example, during his first week in office, President Obama restored funding to organizations that promote and perform abortion overseas. A year later, he signed a health care bill that subsidized insurance plans that fund it here in the United States. At the same time, he rescinded federal regulations that protect doctors from forced participation in elective abortion and threatened to cut off Medicaid funding to any state that denied tax funding to health care entities that provide abortions.[6] Finally, he nominated to the federal courts justices sympathetic to the abortion license whose rulings could set the pro-life cause back for decades to come.

Because ours is a government of the people, Christians have a fundamental duty to work within the political system to limit evil and promote good. Shouldn't social justice start in the womb?

4. Instead of passing laws against abortion, shouldn't pro-life Christians focus on reducing its underlying causes?

First and foremost, the abortion debate turns on the question of human equality. That is, in a nation dedicated to the proposition that all men are created equal, do the unborn count as members of the human family? With that fundamental question in mind, it's unreasonable for liberals to insist that pro-lifers surrender the legal fight to focus on underlying causes. As my colleague Steve Weimar points out, this is like saying the "underlying cause" of spousal abuse is psychological, so instead of making it illegal for husbands to beat their wives, the solution is to provide counseling for men. There are "underlying causes" for rape, murder, theft and so on, but that in no way makes it misguided to have laws banning such actions.[7]

Moreover, why are abortion-defenders even concerned about reducing the number of abortions in the first place? If destroying a human fetus is not a serious moral wrong, why worry about how often it happens? The reason to reduce elective abortion is that human life is unjustly taken—but if that's the case, then restricting the practice makes perfect sense. Imagine a nineteenth-century lawmaker who said that slavery was a bad idea and we ought to reduce it, but owning slaves should remain legal. If those in power adopted his thinking, would this be a good society? True, politics isn't a sufficient answer to injustice, but it's certainly a necessary one. Martin Luther King, Jr., once said, "The law can't make the white man love me, but it can stop him from lynching me."[8] Frankly, if Christians don't think the government-sanctioned killing of unborn children merits a political response, then they misunderstand not only the moral gravity of the situation, but also their mandate to love their neighbor as themselves.

Chapter 19

Making Peace with God

God's gift to the blood-stained conscience is the gospel. Pass it on. Millions of people have been transformed by its message and experienced it as "good news of great joy."

Can God forgive us for shedding innocent blood? Can he forgive us for paying for or supporting someone's decision to end a life? Can he forgive us for saying and doing nothing to stop it? To put the question in context, can God forgive us our abortions and for making peace with child killing?

The question is a derivative of the grand question of sinful people meeting a holy God. Does God forgive sinners? Does God forgive everyone or only some? If God does forgive sinners, on what basis does he forgive? Can God forgive me? How may I experience his mercy and grace for my own sins?

Does the forgiveness of God only go so far? Aren't some things unforgivable? God calls on judges to uphold justice by not condemning the innocent or acquitting the guilty (Exodus 23:6–7). How then can God acquit the guilty and remain just? Does he in the end wink at wickedness and say, "Come on in to my heaven? Let's be buddies!"? Does a rapist and murderer sit down in heaven with the woman he violated and destroyed and say, "Good to see you again, sister, can you pass the bread?" as if nothing happened and nothing needs to be set right? Is that heaven? Or is there hell to pay for our wickedness?

Are there degrees of sin? I'm not a rapist. I am not as bad as (fill in name of mass murdering dictator). How bad are my sins really?

Will God be more inclined to forgive me if I make a sincere effort to reform myself? Will it help if I punish myself in some way? Can I make up for my sins by offsets? Can the rapists then do the same? If so, why was it necessary for Christ to come into the world?

Why is the arrival of Christ announced as "good news of a great joy" (Luke 2:10)? Why did Jesus have to die on the cross? What did Christ accomplish on the cross? How do I experience the benefits of Christ's work personally?

God's one word answer to all these questions is the "gospel." It is through the gospel that we come to experience the grace of God. It's a true conversion experience.

We may be born into a Christian family and raised in the church. But none of us is born a Christian. We become Christians by personally embracing the gospel of Christ. John 1:12–13 says, "To all who received Christ, who believed in his name, he gave the right to become children of God, who were born, not of blood nor of the will of the flesh nor of the will of man, but of God." If the testimonies are true, sometimes this conversion experience happens slowly and over many years. Other times it happens dramatically—almost all at once.

As a result, every Christian has his or her own testimony of what John Newton called amazing grace. "I once was lost but now am found, was blind but now I see."

As a human experience, we repent. From God's perspective, he removes our heart of stone and gives us one that desires to walk with him. As a human experience we "receive" Christ and consciously decide to follow him. From God's perspective, he "calls" sinners and "regenerates" them into his likeness and "adopts" them into his family. Pretty amazing!

C. S. Lewis (1898–1963) described his own starting point. "Amiable agnostics will talk cheerfully about 'man's search for God.' To me, as I then was, they might as well have talked about the mouse's search for the cat."[1] We are all like that. We all seek our own way and live to please ourselves, not God. "All, both Jews and Greeks, are under the power of sin, as it is written: 'None is righteous, no, not one; no one understands; no one seeks for God'" (Romans 3:9–11). Abortion is just one way we tell God to "butt out" of our lives. It is how we declare that we will do what we want, based on what we decide is best for us. Defiance is the common factor in all sin. It is what makes all sin evil: every sin is a rejection of God.

Even what looks like God-seeking behavior—our practice of religion, prior to a change of heart—is more an attempt to buy off God. We go to temple, church, or confession, and offer prayers and perform some community services. But it is akin to a burglar offering a steak to the watch dog—something given to keep God at a safe distance (if that were possible) in order to carry out our plans. Prior to conversion, we are the mouse, and we see God as the cat.

In his *Confessions*, Augustine (354–430) explains why we reach a place where we are ready to make our peace with God. "You have made us for yourself, O Lord, and our hearts are restless until they rest in you." In this classic account of Christian conversion, Augustine describes his own self-centered life and confesses his particular sins of choice. He describes the ebb and flow of the inner battle that we all experience as we undergo conversion. He felt the weight of his guilt and began to see how wretched his sin actually was. But his rebellion against God and his fierce desire to run his own life would reassert itself. He describes how he slowly died to his self-centered life and became alive in Christ. He experienced liberation from sinful habits, freedom from guilt, peace with God, the hope of eternal life, a new heart to serve God and love his neighbors. That's amazing.

This is the gift of God in the gospel. There comes a time in our lives when, like Augustine, Newton, and Lewis, we want to search out and experience the grace of God. We want to know it as a heartfelt, life-changing experience. We want to grasp it intellectually, as something our minds can appreciate and rejoice in. We want to know it as a fortifying power, affecting our decisions and teaching us how to live in a way pleasing to God.

I was in my late teens when I began to pursue God and to take the Christian faith seriously.[2] Through most of my twenties, I was working through the questions above. At the same time, I was helping friends—some struggling specifically with sexual sins and the blood-guilt of abortion—come to a liberating encounter with Christ as well.

You may have a similar experience. You are working through your own faith. And as a student for life, you are interacting with students who are already disgusted and burdened by their choices and ready for a change. They are in need of a life-changing encounter with the forgiveness of God and a new life in Christ.

God's message to all and anyone, regarding any and all of their sins, is the gospel. What then is the gospel?[3]

Paul summarized the "hope of the gospel" in Colossians 1:21–23:

And you, who once were alienated and hostile in mind, doing evil deeds, he has now reconciled in [Christ's] body of flesh by his death, in order to present you holy and blameless and above reproach before him, if indeed you continue in the faith, stable and steadfast, not shifting from the hope of the gospel that you heard, which has been proclaimed in all creation under heaven, and of which I, Paul, became a minister.

This message points to our sin and separation from God, Christ and his death on the cross, and our being made holy and blameless in God's eyes through an abiding and persevering faith in Christ. It affirms that this message is for all of us "under heaven." And it points to an overarching conversion from being an enemy of God to becoming a minister of this gospel.[4] That's amazing.

Put your hope in God. To experience the grace of the gospel, put your hope in God. Our early experiences of the gospel flickers in us as hope. Psalm 147:11 says, "the LORD takes pleasure in those who fear him, in those who hope in his steadfast love." To hope in God is to believe that he exists and that he rewards those who look to him (Hebrews 11:6). To hope in God is to believe that he can forgive and reconcile us to himself, without devaluing his own righteousness, even when we do not see how. To hope in God is to say yes to invitations like this:

Come now, let us reason together, says the LORD:
though your sins are like scarlet,
    they shall be as white as snow;
though they are red like crimson,
    they shall become like wool. (Isaiah 1:18)

To hope in God is to put verses like these on your screen saver:

I will turn their mourning into joy;
   I will comfort them, and give them gladness for
     sorrow (Jeremiah 31:13).

To hope in God is to believe that God had you in mind when he said:

"But this is the covenant that I will make . . . I will put my law within them, and I will write it on their hearts. And I will be their God, and they shall be my people. . . . For I will forgive their iniquity, and I will remember their sin no more " (Jeremiah 31:33–34).

Put your hope in promises like this. Put your hope in God.

Agree with God and confess your sins. Plutarch, the first-century biographer, observed, "Medicine, to produce health, has to examine disease: and music, to create harmony, must investigate discord."[5] In the same way, the gospel requires us to confess our sin and acknowledge that God is right to be angry over our own evil behavior. Agree with God, then, that the reason you feel guilty is because you are guilty. The reason you feel alienated from God is because you are alienated from God (Colossians 1:21). If this were not true, you would not need reconciliation. Whether you feel guilty or not, God says "the wages of sin is death" (Romans 6:23). Believe God more than your feelings.

King David, aflame with lust, stole the wife of another man and then arranged for him to be murdered. David's sexual sins, too, led to the shedding of innocent blood. Our sexual sins and abortions are no different. Therefore, cry out, with David: "For your name's sake, O LORD, pardon my guilt, for it is great" (Psalm 25:11).

Confess in the same way. Don't finesse it by adding self-justifying qualifiers. "Forgive me, Lord, I only did it because (my parents, my boyfriend, my girlfriend, my circumstances were such and such)." This is not asking for forgiveness. This is asking for understanding. David confessed his own true guilt. "Pardon my guilt." He does not say, "Pardon me because it was just a little sin or because I did it only once." He does not minimize it. He admits to the full evil of his own choices. "Pardon me for my sin is great." He does not appeal to offsets as the bases of God's grace, "Look at all the good things I have also done." No, his appeal for mercy is not based on his life, but on God's glory. "For your name's sake, pardon my guilt!"

Agree with God and confess your guilt in prayer. It's painful but it's good pain. C. S. Lewis said, "The hardness of God is kinder than the softness of men, and His compulsion is our liberation."[6]

Look to Christ as your Rescuer. God's promise to pardon and our hope for a miracle in light of the honest confession of our guilt come together in the person and work of Christ. He is the incarnation of God's grace and mercy. As Scripture says, "[God] has delivered us from the domain of darkness and transferred us to the kingdom of his beloved Son, in whom we have redemption, the forgiveness of sins" (Colossians 1:13–14).

We who hope in God look then to Christ. God sent him to rescue and redeem repentant sinners. He is called the "Savior" because he saves us from our sins. He saves us from the just punishment due us for our sin. He saves us from the power of sinful habits. And he delivers us out of the crushing guilt of our past sins. That's amazing.

Trust in the cross. The cross is how God justifies his pardon and mercy. He never winks at sin. God is just and the just wages of sin is death. But the gift of God is Christ dying in our place and suffering the just punishment due us.

> He was pierced for our transgressions;
>   he was crushed for our iniquities;
> upon him was the chastisement that brought us
>   peace,
>   and with his wounds we are healed. (Isaiah 53:5)

That's good news. In putting your faith in Christ's sub-stitutionary death, what are you believing? You are believing first, that Christ died for all your sins, from the least to the ones you are most ashamed of. And second, you are trusting that Christ suffered the full penalty due for each of our sins. That's why it is good news. The cross of Christ is full payment paid for the full penalty due!

And to whom does this apply? To all and anyone who puts their faith in Christ and trusts in the sufficiency of his great work on their behalf. God is just to forgive us. God is free to make peace with us. He is glad to adopt us as his own sons and daughters. Why? Because in Christ, there is no sin left unpunished that could cause God to with-hold his love and friendship toward us. It has all been paid. That is unspeakable joy. That is eternal life.

In case this sounds too good to be true, God raised Jesus from the dead. Acts 17:31 says that God "has given assurance to all by raising [Jesus] from the dead." The res-urrection of Christ is God's stamp of approval or validation that all that Christ did in his life, in his teaching, and in his death on the cross, was acceptable and pleasing to God. Believe, trust, cherish, follow, praise, and keep pursuing Christ. He is risen, and he is ready to live in you from this day forward and through eternity. This is my hope. This is your hope. And this is the message of hope we proclaim to this post-abortion generation. The cross is blood for blood. The cross is Christ's innocent blood shed to cover over your sin of shedding innocent blood. That's good news.

Join, or return to, church, the body of Christ. You would not get married and consider that the end of the matter. In the same way, making peace with God is not the end, but the beginning of a relationship with God. In Christ, you obtain the right to become children of God. You are part of God's family. The visible expression of that family is the church. Yes, I know it has many faults (just like you). But it is God's will for your life. Sticks don't burn unless they are close to each other. The church is God's plan to keep you burning.

For example, guilt tends to return like dandelions. You will need to fight for a clean conscience. Your confidence will grow as your faith and knowledge of Christ grows. That happens by being an active member of a local community of believers dedicated to the word of God and boldly calling you to live out God's purposes for your life.

Chapter 20

Conclusion: Ready, Fire, Aim!

Engage today! You'll learn more along the way.

Ulysses S. Grant was far from perfect, but he changed the course of the Civil War. Unlike other Union generals, he didn't shrink back from the fiercest battles. He engaged them no matter the cost. President Lincoln knew this.

Indeed, when Grant's superiors complained of his alleged vices, Lincoln shot back: "I can't spare this man. He fights!"

Can the pro-life movement spare you?

Like all humans, you've experienced your share of failures, some of which may affect you for years to come. But the answer to your imperfections is not retreat. It's forgiveness. The pro-life cause needs you right now. We are not an elite club of perfect people. We're a company of forgiven sinners who fight injustice. We can't wait for perfection because lives hang in the balance. And that means there's room for you.

Now that you're on campus and know what's at stake, here are five things you can do to engage the pro-life issue. A few of these steps can be done right away with a couple of mouse clicks. Others take more time, but position you for long-term impact. Either way, it's time to get busy!

1. Enlist. Good news! The pro-life movement is exploding on campuses, and you no longer fight alone. Contact Students for Life of America (studentsforlife.org) and determine where your campus pro-life group meets. If there isn't one, ask SFLA to help you start one. At the same time, plan to attend SFLA's annual student conference where you'll meet up with thousands of other students just like you. The conference has grown from just over sixty students in 2003 to more than eighteen hundred in 2011, and it's only getting bigger!

2. Get smart. Elective abortion unjustly takes the life of a defenseless human being, and you must equip yourself to communicate that truth on hostile turf—because that's exactly where you've landed now that you're on campus! In short, you need training! Think of the following as "basic training for your mind."[1]

Start with a few online resources, none of which will cost you a dime. Go to prolifetraining.com and download some pro-life apologetics articles. While you are there, watch Scott's presentation to eighteen hundred students at the 2011 SFLA conference. Then watch his debate with former ACLU president Nadine Strossen at Westmont College. Finally, consider auditing (for free!) the eight-hour pro-life apologetics course he taught at Biola University. You can watch the course online at the following link: http://goo.gl/Vg4Tz. The lecture notes are there as well.

As for books, you don't need to break the bank or overload with tons of additional reading assignments. (Aren't your textbooks enough?) We suggest just two of our own titles to get you started. First, John's *Innocent Blood: Challenging the Powers of Death with the Gospel of Life* (Adelphi, MD: Cruciform Press, 2011) will give you a theological foundation for approaching campus ministry groups—many of which do not see the connection between the pro-life movement and biblical truth. Second, Scott's book, *The Case for Life: Equipping Christians to Engage the Culture* (Wheaton, IL: Crossway, 2009), will give you tools to graciously defend your pro-life beliefs on hostile turf.

3. Show some heart. All over campus are young women who recently got some very disturbing news from a pregnancy test. The men in their lives may not be there to support them, but you can. First, contact your local pregnancy help center and ask what can be done to assist these young women. If the pregnancy center needs someone to man a booth on campus, do it. If it's attacked in the school newspaper, write a rebuttal. When the center hosts its annual fundraising banquet, volunteer to help serve. Second, contact Students for Life of America and inquire about its Pregnant on Campus initiative (studentsforlife.org). Ask if the local pregnancy help center is aware of that initiative and how the two groups can work together to reach more women.

4. Vote to save lives. What does a pro-life vote look like? At the executive level (president, governors), it's easy. Vote for the candidate who will do his or her best to legally protect unborn humans.

But what about the legislative level, where the choice is not so simple? Here's the short answer: In a nation where the people are the government, pro-life Christians have a duty to apply their biblical worldview in a way that limits evil and promotes the good insofar as possible given current political realities. At the legislative level in particular (House and Senate races), that usually means voting for the party that, though imperfect, will best protect unborn humans against one that sanctions killing them. The reason is simple: at the legislative level, political parties, more than individuals, determine which laws see the light of day.

Consider the House of Representatives. If a party committed to elective abortion controls the chamber, it will squash pro-life bills and promote pro-abortion ones. Even if that pro-abortion party has a few pro-life members, those members will likely never get to vote on a pro-life bill unless their party is not in power!

But it gets worse. These same pro-life members of that pro-abortion party almost always put party politics above moral principle when it comes to the most important vote they will cast—selection of the speaker. Remember, the speaker of the House ultimately determines the legislative agenda, and if the party committed to elective abortion controls the chamber, its candidate for speaker will inevitably be pro-abortion. Nevertheless, these pro-life members vote for their party's candidate for speaker, which all but guarantees that pro-life bills never see the light of day. In most cases, then, they aren't reforming their party's pro-abortion stance; they're enabling it!

Perhaps you worry that voting for a non-pro-life candidate in a larger pro-life party constitutes cooperation with evil. After all, you are voting for someone who supports abortion, even though his party is pro-life and will advance pro-life bills. At this point, we need to distinguish between formal cooperation with evil and material cooperation with it. In the first case, you intend to enable evil. In the second, you intend no such thing, only to limit an even greater evil act—thus, you do not share in the guilt. To borrow an example from J. Budziszewski, suppose you're a teller at the local bank when a gunman grabs a hostage and says, "Give me the money in the drawer or I'll blow his head off." Should you give him the cash? Of course you should. True, in doing so, you assist him in the theft, but that is not your intent. You're not trying to help him do wrong. Rather, your intention is to keep him from committing an even graver moral wrong, murder![2]

In the same way, when you vote in the general election for a non-pro-life candidate of a pro-life party, you don't share in the guilt of the wrong things he wants to do once elected. You don't intend his wrong actions, only to prevent an even greater harm—the empowering of a party which favors setting aside an entire class of human beings to be killed!

If parties drive legislation, how should pro-life students educate Christians on the relationship between politics and biblical morality? First, they should teach a biblical worldview affirming that all humans have value because they bear the image of their maker. Second, they should challenge Christians to live out that biblical view in every area of their lives, including their political affiliations. Third, they should stress that while no political party is perfect, on the question of fundamental human value, some parties are more in line with biblical truth than others.

Suppose, for example, that it's 1860 and 50 percent of professing Christians in your campus fellowship group are members of a political party dedicated to the proposition that an entire class of human beings can be enslaved or killed to meet the needs of the white race. If you're a Christian leader committed to applying a biblical worldview in all areas of life, is this okay? You might be sympathetic to new converts coming to grips with Christian teaching, but mature Christians? True, campus ministries can't use their resources to endorse political candidates or parties, but they can (and must) teach that a biblical worldview informs our political behavior—including which parties we choose to empower with our vote. Saying so is not wrong—it's leadership.

5. Engage those who should be with us but aren't. Those involved with InterVarsity, Cru (formerly known as Campus Crusade), Navigators, and various Baptist or Catholic student organizations are fellow students who share your worldview, but do not understand your passion for life. In fact, our experience is that these groups often fail to join in any pro-life activities. Why?

First, the word "pro-life" has many negative overtones attached to it. When people hear pro-life, they often think rude, confrontational, even violent.

Second, Christian groups, especially evangelical ones, shy away out of a fundamental misunderstanding that abortion is a political issue while they see themselves as nonpolitical. They are about changing hearts. They think you are about changing laws. Of course, we are much more involved in changing hearts and minds than anything else, but this is the perception we must correct.

Third, Christian groups see their primary mission as evangelism. They do see the linkage between abortion and the gospel.

How can you build bridges to Christian groups on campus?

First, build relationships. It's always a mistake to wait until your pro-life event is planned and then reach out to other Christian groups. Instead, make it your mission at the beginning of every school year to build friendships in these groups by attending their meetings and events. Then you will be inviting friends to your event.

Second, start with the Bible and your testimony, not with the activism. Evangelical groups are keen on asking biblical questions and discussing matters faith and action. So raise biblical questions like, "How do we obey Proverbs 24:10–12 today?" Then share your story of how you are answering this call, or hope to. Share your journey to getting active.

Third, "I regret my abortion" are the four most powerful words at your disposal. Bring them forward. The testimony of fellow students who have experienced the agony of abortion personally will start a fire of concern in your fellow Christian students. It is God's chief way of helping people see the links between abortion and the urgent need of God's grace in the gospel, and the lifesaving, death-defying power of neighborly love.

Final thought: Before Ulysses S. Grant assumed command of the Union army, it would venture south into Confederate territory, suffer a defeat, then withdraw northward to conduct endless marching drills and meaningless grand reviews—anything to avoid striking a serious blow at the enemy.

That all changed when Lincoln put Grant in charge. Journalist Michael Kilian describes the immediate impact the new general made on an army conditioned to defeat:

> In May 1864 . . . a horrible, two-day battle ensued, with many wounded burning to death when the woods caught fire. The fight was a standoff but so costly to the North a Union withdrawal was expected.
>
> On the rainy night after the close of battle, the weary soldiers of the battered Union Army were slogging along, believing they were once again going to retreat, as they had done time after time in Virginia since the first battle of Bull Run three years before.

Instead, at the crossroads, they encountered the muddy, unkempt figure of their new commanding general, who sat upon his horse, blocking the road to the north, directing the troops onto another that led south and east and eventually to Richmond.[3]

President Lincoln couldn't spare Grant, and the pro-life movement can't spare you. The campus environment is hostile and deceptive. Many of our Christian leaders have long since abandoned the fight. Our campus ministry groups do precious little equipping pro-life apologists to defend a biblical worldview on abortion. And there's no question that political leadership has disappointed us on many fronts.

But quitting is not an option.

Consider this book your enlistment papers. The authors, much older than you and veterans of many pro-life battles, know the challenges awaiting you. We've taken our hits and learned things along the way. We will never retire from the pro-life movement until our commanding general summons us home.

Till then, we stand at the crossroads pointing you toward victory.

About the Authors

John Ensor

John Ensor is the president of PassionLife, a global missions initiative to spread the gospel of life and expand the pregnancy help movement in countries suffering the highest abortion rates in the world. John is an evangelical pastor who has served the pregnancy help movement in the U.S. for more than twenty years, as a leader, speaker, writer, trainer, and co-laborer.

John and his wife, Kristen, have been married thirty-three years. They have three grown children, two daughters-in-law, and three grandchildren. They live in Rowell, Georgia.

To learn more visit: passionlife.org

Contact John or invite him to your campus at: http://johnensor.com/contact/requestinfo

Other Books by John Ensor

The Great Work of the Gospel: How We Experience God's Grace. Wheaton, IL: Crossway, 2006.

Doing Things Right in Matters of the Heart. Wheaton, IL: Crossway, 2007.

Answering the Call: Saving Innocent Lives, One Woman at a Time. Peabody, MA: Hendrickson Publishers, 2011.

Innocent Blood: Challenging the Powers of Death with the Gospel of Life. Adelphi, MD: Cruciform Press, 2011.

Scott Klusendorf

Scott Klusendorf is the president of Life Training Institute, where he trains pro-life advocates to persuasively defend their views. A passionate and engaging platform speaker, Scott's pro-life presentations have been featured by Students for Life of America, Focus on the Family, Truths That Transform, and American Family Radio. Scott routinely debates abortion-choice advocates at the university level, and his book *The Case for Life: Equipping Christians to Engage the Culture* (Crossway, 2009) gives pro-life students the tools they need to stand their ground. Scott is a graduate of UCLA and holds an M.A. in Christian apologetics from Biola University.

To learn more, visit Scott's website:
www.prolifetraining.com

If you'd like Scott to speak at your campus, call Life Training Institute at 719-264-7861.

Notes

Introduction

1. Some pro-life materials use the modifier *preborn*, rather than unborn child. We like it, since it presupposes the humanity of the child in a way that unborn child does not. But in this book, we use the term *unborn* for two reasons. First, we do not feel it in any way dehumanizes the child, since it's an accurate description of the child's status. Second, we want to help you make the case for life, rather than beg the question.

2. See Rodney Stark, *For the Glory of God: How Monotheism Led to Reformations, Science, Witch-Hunts and the End of Slavery* (Princeton, NJ: Princeton University Press, 2003).

Chapter 1: Defending Your Pro-Life Views in Five Minutes or Less

1. For more on this see, Gregory Koukl, *Precious Unborn Human Persons* (Lomita, CA: STR Press, 1999), 11.

2. See T. W. Sadler, *Langman's Embryology*, 5th ed. (Philadelphia: W. B. Saunders, 1993), 3; Ronand O'Rahilly and Pabiola Muller, *Human Embryology and Teratology*, 2nd ed. (New York: Wiley-Liss, 1996), 8, 29.

3. Keith L. Moore and T. V. N. Persaud, *The Developing Human: Clinically Oriented Embryology* (Philadelphia: W. B. Saunders, 1998), 2.

4. A. Guttmacher, *Life in the Making: The Story of Human Procreation* (New York: Viking, 1933), 3.

5. Stephen Schwarz, *The Moral Question of Abortion* (Chicago: Loyola University Press, 1990), 18.

Chapter 2: Understanding Why We Speak of the Sanctity of Life

1. Bernard Nathanson, "Confessions of an Ex-abortinist," About Abortions, http://www.aboutabortions.com/Confess.html.

2. He was one of three founders of the National Association for the Repeal of Abortion Laws (later renamed the National

Abortion Rights Action League and now known as NARAL Pro-Choice America). To read his own account, see Bernard Nathanson, *Aborting America* (Garden City, NY: Doubleday, 1979).

3. "Q and A with Bernard Nathanson," *Focus on the Family Citizen* (August 26, 1996): 7.

4. Bernard Nathanson, *The Hand of God* (Washington, DC: Regnery, 1996), 19.

5. See "Maternal Bonding in Early Fetal Ultrasound," *The New England Journal of Medicine*, February 17, 1983.

6. Lydia Saad, "More Americans 'Pro-Life' than 'Pro-Choice' for the First Time," Gallup Politics, May 15, 2009, http://www.gallup.com/poll/118399/more-americans-pro-life-than-pro-choice-first-time.aspx.

7. John Jefferson Davis, *Abortion and the Christian* (Phillipsburg, N.J.: Presbyterian and Reformed Publishing, 1984), p. 40.

8. Clifford Bajema, *Abortion and the Meaning of Personhood* (Grand Rapids, MI: Baker, 1974), 32.

Chapter 3: Simplifying the Abortion Debate in a Moral Fog

1. I owe this illustration to Greg Koukl, *Precious Unborn Human Persons* (Lomita, CA: STR Press, 1998), 7.

2. Ibid.

3. Francis J. Beckwith, *Defending Life: A Moral and Legal Case against Abortion Choice* (New York: Cambridge University Press, 2007), 94–95.

Chapter 4: Developing a Christian Response to Abortion

1. Some might object that since Christians are under the New Covenant, the Old Testament commands no longer apply. True, Jesus fulfilled the Mosaic Law, but where he affirms it, believers have an obligation to obey. In Matthew 5:21 Jesus affirms the prohibition against shedding innocent blood.

2. Eva Fogalman, *Conscience and Courage: Rescuers of Jews during the Holocaust* (New York: G. P. Putnam's, 1951), 70.

3. Corrie ten Boom, *The Hiding Place* (New York: Bantam Books, 1974), 99.

Chapter 5: Clarifying Right and Wrong in a Relative World

1. Francis J. Beckwith and Gregory Koukl, *Relativism: Feet Firmly Planted in Mid-Air* (Grand Rapids, MI: Baker Books, 1998), 36–39.

2. Greg Dickinson, "Anti-abortion campaign at Hornbake pushes moral convictions on students," letter printed in University of Maryland paper after a Genocide Awareness Project event in October 2003.

3. Greg Koukl, "Interview with Summit Ministries," *Solid Ground*, September–October 1998.

4. C. S. Lewis, *Mere Christianity* (New York: Touchstone, 1996), 19.

5. *Planned Parenthood v. Casey*, 505 U.S. 833, at 851 (1992).

Chapter 6: Converting Your Heritage into Your Legacy

1. Phillip Hallie, *Lest Innocent Blood Be Shed* (New York: Harper Perennial, 1994).

2. Ibid., 3.

3. Ibid., 194.

4. George Grant, *Third Time Around: A History of the Pro-Life Movement from the First Century to the Present* (Brentwood, TN: Wolgemuth & Hyatt, 1991), 12.

5. Clayton Jefford, ed., *The Didache in Context, Essays on Its Text, History and Transmission* (Leiden: E. J. Brill, 1995), 1.1; 2.2.

6. Quoted from Michael Gorman, *Abortion and the Early Church* (Eugene, OR: Wipf and Stock, 1982), 59–60.

7. Augustine, *On Marriage and Concupiscence* 1:17.15.

8. Quoted in Grant, *Third Time Around*, 21.

9. Ibid., 21.

10. Ibid., 38.

11. John Calvin, in "Bearing the Cross, A Part of Self-Denial," *The Institutes of the Christian Religion in 2 Vol.,* ed. John T. McNeil, in The Library of Christian Classics, vol. 20 (Philadelphia: Westminster Press, 1977), 707.

12. Lambert Collier, *The Jesuits: The Warrior Priests of the Pope* (New York: Maethan Brothers, 1926), 87.

13. Quoted in Grant, *Third Time Around*, 53.

14. Vishal Mangalwadi and Ruth Mangalwadi, *The Legacy of William Carey: A Model for the Transformation of a Culture* (Wheaton, IL: Crossway, 1993), 17–25.

15. Ibid., 33.

16. Quoted in Charles Colson, *Kingdoms in Conflict* (Grand Rapids, MI: Zondervan, 1987), 101.

Chapter 7: Keeping Cool under Fire

1. Gregory Koukl, "Tactics in Defending the Faith" lecture notes. Order from Stand to Reason, www.str.org. Portions of the chapter adapted from Scott Klusendorf, *The Case for Life: Equipping Christians to Engage the Culture* (Wheaton, IL: Crossway, 2009), 149–156.

2. Ibid. The material in this section is adapted from Koukl's "Tactics in Defending the Faith."

3. Gregory Koukl, "Take a Tip from Lt. Columbo," Stand to Reason's *Solid Ground,* November-December 1999, http://www.str.org/site/News2?page=NewsArticle&id=5621.

Chapter 8: Winning with Winsomeness

1. You can watch Scott debate former ACLU president Nadine Strossen at Westmont College. He is firm but charitable. Learn from this example. "Abortion Debate at Westmont College," http://vimeo.com/26031452.

2. Norma McCorvey with Gary Thomas, "Roe v. McCorvey," Roe No More Ministry, http://www.leaderu.com/norma/nmtestimony.html.

3. Ibid.

4. Ibid.

5. Ibid.

6. Ibid.

7. Norma McCorvey with Gary Thomas, *Won by Love* (Nashville: Thomas Nelson, 1997).

8. For example, Dr. Bernard Nathanson (see chap. 2) was converted to the life position in the seventies but won to Christ through the active witness of the Christian pro-life community. See Bernard Nathanson, *The Hand of God* (Washington, DC: Regnery, 1996). More recently Abby Johnson, in *Unplanned* (Wheaton, IL: Tyndale House, 2011), testifies that she migrated from being a volunteer escort in 2001 at the Planned Parenthood business in Byron, Texas, to their

"Employee of the Year" in 2008, to an advocate for life and a Christian in 2009. A few loving pro-life Christians played a significant role.

Chapter 9: Rape and Abortion

1. Francis Beckwith uses this example in *Politically Correct Death: Answering Arguments for Abortion Rights* (Grand Rapids, MI: Baker Books, 1993), 69.

2. Akinrinola Bankole, Susheela Singh, and Taylor Haas, "Reasons Why Women Have Induced Abortions: Evidence from 27 Countries," *International Family Planning Perspectives* 24, no. 3 (September 1998).

Chapter 10: Listening to the Victims of Sexual Assault

1. Kathleen DeZeeuw, quoted in *Victims and Victors,* ed. David Reardon, Julie Makimaa, and Amy Sobie (Springfield, IL: Acorn Books, 2000), see Elliot Institute, http://afterabortion.org/2005/victims-and-victors-speaking-out-about-their-pregnancies-abortions-and-children-resulting-from-sexual-assault/.

2. David C. Reardon, "Rape, Incest and Abortion: Searching beyond the Myths," Elliot Institute, http://afterabortion.org/2004/rape-incest-and-abortion-searching-beyond-the-myths-3/.

3. See Sandra K. Mahkorn, "Pregnancy and Sexual Assault," in *The Psychological Aspects of Abortion,* ed. David Mall and Walter Watts (Washington, DC, University Publications of America, 1979), pp. 55–69. Reardon's own study found 73 percent birth rate among the 164 pregnant rape victims he interviewed. See David Reardon, Julie Makimaa, and Amy Sobie, eds., *Victims and Victors* (Springfield, IL: Acorn Books, 2000).

4. David C. Reardon, *Aborted Women, Silent No More* (Chicago: Loyola University Press, 1987), 206.

5. Reardon, "Rape, Incest and Abortion."

6. I highly recommend reading Heather Gemmen's personal account of being raped at knifepoint, seeking out an abortion at first, then slowly but surely coming to see the hand of Goodness triumphing over the evil she endured. See Heather Gemmen, *Startling Beauty: My Journey from Rape to Restoration* (Colorado Springs: Life Journey, 2004).

7. Received in a donor support letter, Spring 2011.

Chapter 11: What about Back-Alley Abortions

1. This appeared on the NOW website on July 5, 2005.

2. "Anti-abortion Chain Marks Roe v. Wade Anniversary," *The Oakland Press*, January 22, 2007.

3. Francis J. Beckwith, *Politically Correct Death: Answering Arguments for Abortion Rights* (Grand Rapids: Baker Books, 1993), 55.

4. Mary Anne Warren, "On the Moral and Legal Status of Abortion," in *The Problem of Abortion*, ed. Joel Feinberg (Belmont, CA: Wadsworth, 1984).

5. "An Objective Model for Estimating Criminal Abortions and Its Implications for Public Policy," cited in *New Perspectives on Human Abortion*, ed. Thomas W. Hilgers, Dennis J. Horan, and David Mall (Frederick, MD: University Publications of America, 1981), 78.

6. "Current Trends Abortion Surveillance: Preliminary Analysis—United States, 1981," *Morbidity and Mortality Weekly Report*, Centers for Disease Control, July 6, 1984.

7. Greg Koukl, "I'm Pro-Choice," Stand to Reason, http://www.str.org/site/News2?page=NewsArticle&id=5313.

8. Mary S. Calderone, "Illegal Abortion as a Public Health Problem," *American Journal of Public Health*, July 1960.

9. *Morbidity and Mortality Weekly Report*, Centers for Disease Control Surveillance Summaries, September 5, 1992, 33.

10. Daniel Callahan, *Abortion: Law, Choice, and Morality* (New York: Macmillan, 1970), 132–136.

Chapter 12: What about Abortion to Save the Mother's Life?

1. Akinrinola Bankole, Susheela Singh, and Taylor Haas, "Reasons Why Women Have Induced Abortions: Evidence from 27 Countries," *International Family Planning Perspectives* 24, no. 3, September 1998.

2. Warren Hern, *Abortion Practice* (Boulder, CO: Alpenglo Graphics, 1990), 10, 39.

3. T. E. Goldner, H. W. Lawson, Z. Xia, and H. K. Atrash, "Surveillance for Ectopic Pregnancy—United States, 1970–1989," in *Morbidity and Mortality Weekly Report*, Centers for Disease Control Surveillance Summaries, December 1993; 42 (no. SS-6), 73–85.

4. Eric Daiter, M.D., "Ectopic Pregnancy: Overview," UBM Medica, http://www.obgyn.net/women/women.asp?page=/pb/cotm/9902/9902.

5. Christopher Kaczor, "The Ethics of Ectopic Pregnancy: A Critical Reconsideration of Salpingostomy and Methotrexate," *Linacre Quarterly*, August 2009.

6. As a result, some pro-life advocates think we should avoid the term *abortion* in this case because the intent is radically different from abortions performed for socioeconomic reasons.

7. Kaczor, "Ethics of Ectopic Pregnancy."

8. Thomas Murphy Goodwin, "Medicalizing Abortion Decisions," *First Things* (March 1996): 33–36.

Chapter 13: Cross Bearing for the Child Bearing

1. Paul Swope, "Abortion: A Failure to Communicate," *First Things* (April 1998): 31–35, www.firstthings.com/article/2008/11/004-abortion-a-failure-to-communicate-49.

2. Source: "A List of Major Physical Complications of Abortion," Elliot Institute, http://afterabortion.org/1999/abortion-risks-a-list-of-major-physical-complications-related-to-abortion.

3. Paul C. Reisser, M.D., and Teri K. Reisser, M.S., "Identifying and Overcoming Post-Abortion Syndrome," (Colorado Springs: Focus on the Family, 1994), 11.

4. They did get married. I did the wedding.

Chapter 14: What about the Mantra "My Body, My Choice"?

1. Judith Jarvis Thomson, "A Defense of Abortion," *Philosophy and Public Affairs* 1 (1971).

2. Stephen Schwarz, *The Moral Question of Abortion* (Chicago: Loyola University Press, 1990), 118.

3. Gregory Koukl, "Unstringing the Violinist," Stand to Reason, http://www.str.org/site/News2?page=NewsArticle&id=5689.

4. Schwarz, *Moral Question of Abortion*, 122.

5. Ibid., 116.

6. Francis J. Beckwith, *Politically Correct Death: Answering Arguments for Abortion Rights* (Grand Rapids, MI: Baker Books, 1993), 133.

7. Rich Poupard, "Do No Harm (Except for the Killing Thing)," blogpost, http://lti-blog.blogspot.com/2007/01/do-no-harm-except-for-that-killing.html.

8. Jonathan Turley, "When Choice Becomes Tyranny: Abortion Rights Lobby Steps Over the Line in Utah," *Jewish World Review*, March 23, 2004.

Chapter 15: Revealing the Truth about Abortion

1. Bernard Nathanson, *The Abortion Papers* (New York: Frederick Fell, 1983), 170.

2. Nathanson estimates that he is responsible for 75,000 abortions and confesses that he personally aborted his own child. He also wrote, "In the mid-sixties I impregnated a woman . . . and I not only demanded that she terminate the pregnancy . . . but also coolly informed her that since I was one of the most skilled practitioners of the art, I myself would do the abortion. And I did." Bernard Nathanson, *The Hand of God* (Washington, DC: Regnery, 1996), 58–59.

3. Kim Flodin, "Why I Don't March." My Turn, *Newsweek*, February 12, 1990, 8.

4. Lambert Collier, *The Jesuits: The Warrior Priests of the Pope* (New York: Maethan Brothers, 1926), 87.

Chapter 16: If Men Can't Get Pregnant, Should They Speak Up about Abortion?

1. Francis J. Beckwith, *Politically Correct Death* (Grand Rapids, MI: Baker Books, 1993), 90.

Chapter 17: Manning Up!

1. "Men and Women Hold Similar Views on the Legality of Abortion," Public Agenda, http://www.publicagenda.org/charts/men-and-women-hold-similar-views-legality-abortion.

2. A 1994 Roper poll revealed that 48 percent of men favored a more pro-abortion position, while only 40 percent of women did so. In a 1998 Writhlin poll, women consistently expressed a more pro-life position (61 percent) than did men (53 percent).

3. Quoted by Richard Stith "Her Body, Her Problem" *First Things*, August–September 2009, http://www.firstthings.com/article/2009/07/her-choice-her-problem.

4. Quoted by Serrin Foster, in "The Feminist Case against Abortion," *The American Feminist* 11, nos. 2–3 (Summer–Fall 2004), http://www.feministsforlife.org/taf/2004/summer-fall/Summer-Fall04.pdf, 30.

5. David C. Reardon, *Aborted Women, Silent No More* (Chicago: Loyola University Press, 1997), 31.

6. Frederica Mathewes-Green, *Real Choices: Offering Practical, Life-Affirming Alternatives to Abortion* (Sisters, OR: Multnomah, 1994), 248.

7. Reardon, *Aborted Women, Silent No More*, 11.

8. P. G. Ney, T. Fung, A. R. Wickett, and C. Beaman-Dodd, "The Effects of Pregnancy Loss on Women's Health," *Journal of Science and Medicine* 38 (1994): 1193–1200.

9. Wendy Shalit, *A Return to Modesty* (New York: Touchstone, 1999), 8.

10. Quoted in Foster, "Feminist Case against Abortion," 29–30.

11. Quoted in ibid., 29.

12. No doubt there are circumstances in which a happily married wife can become abortion vulnerable. But this is rare. Most women resort to abortion because they lack the support found in a stable marriage.

13. If you want to explore a Christian approach to dating, love, and marriage, I think you will enjoy reading my thoughts and experiences in John Ensor, *Doing Things Right in Matters of the Heart* (Wheaton, IL: Crossway, 2007).

14. Sexual purity outside of marriage makes for sexual passion within marriage. An entire book of the Bible, the Song of Solomon, is devoted to affirming the intimate passion of marital love.

15. Shalit, *A Return to Modesty*, 93.

Chapter 18: Is War Worse than Abortion?

1. For an evangelical example, see "Interview with Donald Miller," Burnside Writer's Blog entry, August 25, 2008, http://burnsidewriterscollective.blogspot.com/2008/09/interview-with-donald-miller.html. For a Catholic example, see Michael New, "Professors Robert George and Douglas Kmiec Debate Abortion, a Pro-Life Recap," *Life News*, June 1, 2009.

2. Alex Spillius, "Barack Obama Doubles Support from Evangelical Christians" *The Telegraph*, November 7, 2008.

3. Francis J. Beckwith, "Why Reducing the Number of Abortions Is Not Necessarily Pro-Life," *Moral Accountability*, February 12, 2009, http://www.moralaccountability.com/2009/02/12/why-reducing-the-number-of-abortions-not-necessarily-prolife/%.

4. See Randy Alcorn (EMP Blog, November 16, 2008) and Steve Hays (Triablogue, January 30, 2006) for more.

5. Helen Alvare et al., "The Lazy Slander of the Pro-Life Cause," *Public Discourse*, January 17, 2011; Arthur C. Brooks, "A Nation of Givers," *The American*, March–April 2008.

6. O. Carter Snead, "Protect the Weak and Vulnerable: The Primacy of the Life Issue," *Public Discourse*, August 22, 2011.

7. Scott Klusendorf, The Case for Life: Equipping Christians to Engage the Culture (Wheaton, IL: Crossway, 2009), 169.

8. Speech at Western Michigan University, December 18, 1963.

Chapter 19: Making Peace with God

1. C. S. Lewis, *Surprised by Joy* (New York: Harcourt, Brace & World, 1955), 227.

2. Prior to this, if you had asked me, "Are you a Christian?" I would have surely said yes. But I would mean this only in a cultural sense, that I am not a Jew or a Muslim, that I attend a church and not a temple, that I believe God exists, that I like the Christmas story. But I would not mean that I love God and desire to know him and do his will. That is precisely what was missing in my Christian experience up until my late teens.

3. Our aim is to introduce the essential truths of the gospel as conveyed in the Bible and testified to in power by the millions of transformed lives left in its wake down through the centuries (including the lives of the authors). While various traditions within the church disagree on points of emphasis, order, definition, language, and relationship between these truths, we think what is presented here reflects the historic orthodox understanding of the gospel. We encourage you to consult your own tradition, discuss these truths with other believers, read widely, and most of all, examine the Scriptures for yourself.

4. Paul's own conversion is told in Acts 9. Acts 22:1–21 records Paul's own testimony, and you can see how he experienced each of these converting steps—how he went from enemy of Christ to a proclaimer of the gospel.

5. Famous Quotes, http://www.famousquotes.com/author/plutarch/2.

6. Lewis, *Surprised by Joy*, 229.

Chapter 20: Conclusion: Ready, Fire, Aim!

1. I owe this catchy phrase to Greg Koukl.

2. J. Budziszewski, "Ballot Box Blues," *Boundless*, October 28, 2004, http://www.boundless.org/2005/articles/a0000958.cfm.

3. Michael Kilian, "Grant's Two Wars: On the Trail of the Union's Greatest General," *Chicago Tribune*, May 20, 2002.